1001 *Beastly* BODY FACTS

1001 Beastly BODY FACTS

Helen Otway

ARCTURUS

This edition published in 2009 by Arcturus Publishing Limited
26/27 Bickels Yard, 151–153 Bermondsey Street,
London SE1 3HA

ISBN: 978-1-84837-228-3
CH000494EN

Editor: Fiona Tulloch
Cover goblin illustration by Steve Beaumont
Design and illustration by Dynamo Ltd

Printed in Singapore

CONTENTS

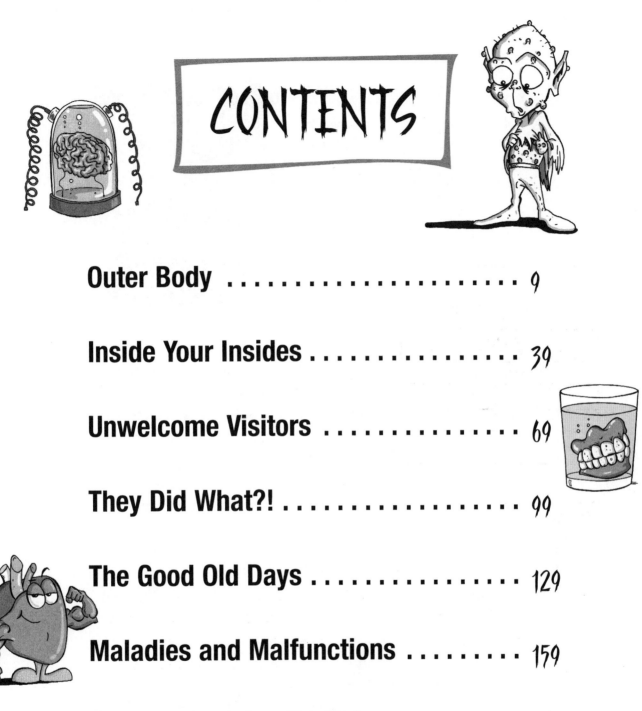

1001 *Beastly* BODY FACTS

How amazing is your body? Even as you sit quietly reading this, it's still a hive of non-stop activity – your super-strong heart muscle is pumping blood, your digestive system is processing whatever you ate recently and your skin is busy renewing itself, especially if you have any bruises or scabs! Have you noticed that you can't stay very still for long, too? That's because every so often, your brain will make your muscles shift various parts of your body into a different position to keep you comfortable.

Everybody's body is amazing without really doing much; but the body is also capable of incredible feats: 43 world records were broken when 10,500 athletes competed at the 2008 Olympic Games in Beijing and pushed their bodies to the limit in their quest to swim, run, cycle or row faster than ever before. If you fancy having a record-breaking body yourself, you don't have to be an Olympic athlete – you could just try juggling with 11 balls, knitting 118 stitches in one minute, or doing 177,737 pogo jumps to get yourself in the record books!

Amazing survivors

Some people don't realize how amazing their bodies are until they find themselves in the most difficult of circumstances and have to fight for survival. Here are just a couple of examples…

German teenager Juliane Köpke was a passenger on an aeroplane that was shot to pieces by lightning over the Amazonian rainforest in 1971. Still strapped to her seat, she was the only one to survive the fall. She spent the following nine days wading down a stream in search of civilization and eventually came across some lumbermen, who treated her injuries and bug infestations as best they could before taking her on the seven-hour journey to safety.

Nineteenth-century American frontiersman Hugh Glass was badly mauled by a grizzly bear and abandoned by his fellow hunters, who were convinced he would die of his injuries. He set his own broken leg, used maggots to clean his festering wounds and wrapped himself in a bear hide to keep warm so he could manage the six-week crawl to the nearest settlement.

If you want to find out about the amazing, mind-boggling and beastly things your body is capable of without risking your life, then read on...

Don't try this at home!

Your body is amazing and you need to keep it that way. If you want to become a performing flatulist to entertain your friends, then good luck; if you want to keep your belly button fluff in a jar, that's fine too (if you don't mind losing those friends). What you really mustn't do, though, is try any of the risky stuff that you read about in this book. So-called achievements like swimming under ice and scoffing television sets are done by crazy adults who have undergone endless hours of special training, mainly because they have nothing better to do. Don't try to copy them – find safer ways to amuse yourself instead!

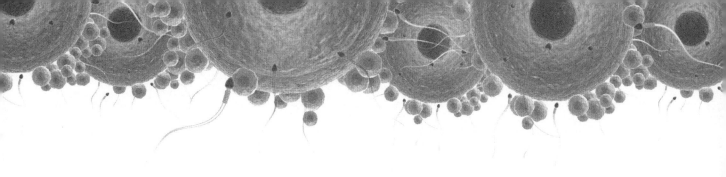

Outer Body

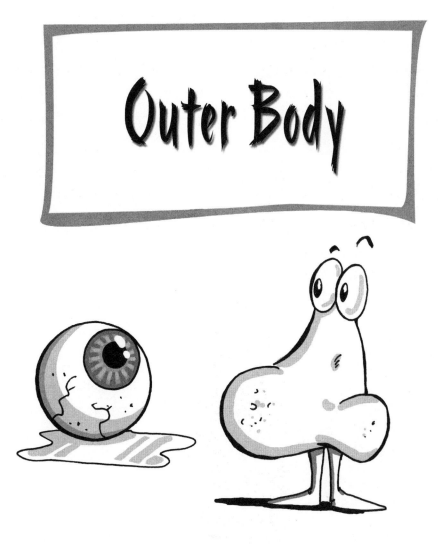

When you sneeze, the air coming out of your nose and mouth travels at the same speed as a category 2 hurricane: 160 kilometres/100 miles an hour!

Your sense of smell is 10,000 times more sensitive than your sense of taste. About 80 per cent of what you taste comes from what you can smell, which is why you don't taste much at all if you have a cold!

Your fingerprints were formed six months before you were born.

Earwax tastes very bitter. If you must try it, make sure no one's looking...

British man Graham Butterfield has such a sensitive bottom that he tests beds for a living. He has insured his behind for £1 million/US$1.4 million!

Your body makes a new skin every month – that means you'll get through about 1,000 skins in your lifetime!

Most of the world's population has brown eyes. In the US, only one person in six has blue eyes, compared to every other person a century ago. Where did all those blue eyes go?!

Some perfumes contain *ambergris*. Sounds nice? It's whale vomit!

In space, astronauts use specially formulated non-toxic toothpaste, because they have to swallow all the froth. Gross!

You sweat all day long, even when you don't feel it. As you read this, more than two million sweat glands around your body are working to keep it at the right temperature.

What you hear when you fart is the vibration of your sphincter muscles as air passes through them. The sort of sound you get depends on how fast the air is travelling.

Poisons can give you great-looking skin! *Botulinum toxin* (Botox) is famous for its wrinkle-smoothing effects, but for those who don't like needles there is a cream that mimics viper venom and gives similar results.

Touch signals travel to the brain more quickly than pain signals. That's why you feel the bump from stubbing your toe before the agony sets in!

When you were born, you couldn't see further than the end of your nose.

The first modern dental floss was invented in 1815. It was made of silk!

Your fingertips and lips are packed with touch sensors, making them the most sensitive parts of your body.

If you cut yourself, your body will produce one million extra cells an hour until it heals.

Fancy a Japanese bird poop facial? The special enzymes in the droppings of the Japanese Bush Warbler make it an ingredient in some anti-wrinkle and skin-whitening treatments.

Chin dimples are hereditary.

You produce a lot of saliva – about 1 litre/2 pints a day. A cow produces 200 times more!

You have more bacteria on your body than there are people in the world.

Yawning is your body's way of getting more oxygen into your lungs to try and make you feel more awake.

Your eye muscles just can't keep still – they move more than 100,000 times a day and are even busy while you're asleep!

Cola is more acidic than vinegar…and acid destroys the enamel on your teeth, so remember to brush properly!

The most bizarre cosmetic procedure has to be tongue-splitting: a scalpel or laser is used to cut down the middle of the tongue and give it a forked appearance. Freaky!

The Achilles tendon, at the back your foot, is named after a mythological Greek hero.

Nose-pickings are a mixture of dried mucus and what is filtered out of the air you breathe – pollen, dust, fungus, dirt, maybe the odd bug and even tiny particles of dust from space!

Your fingerprints, palm prints, tongue print, toe prints and sole prints are all unique!

Your sense of hearing is at its best when you are ten years old.

Inside each eye you have a clear lens just behind your pupil. These lenses yellow slightly as you get older, affecting your perception of blue light. So if your granny thinks your black jumper is really blue, she hasn't gone mad – it's just her eyes!

Sweat is made mainly of water, so it doesn't smell…until it's been around a while. Once skin bacteria have had time to slurp it up and multiply, the whiff begins.

A sheet of skin can be grown from just a few of your cells. New skin is grown in special laboratories and used to replace damaged skin in a skin graft operation.

Humans live longer than any other mammals on the planet.

Your tear ducts go from your eyes to your nose. That's why your nose runs when you cry and why you can sometimes taste eye drops.

Over your lifetime, you will spend a whole two weeks kissing. Yes, you will!

Austrian man Martin Bierbauer claimed damages after he was blasted off his toilet by hailstones during a freak storm. A council spokesman admitted that blocked drains were to blame.

Each of your taste buds lasts for just a week! They are most quickly replaced when you are young.

Fair-haired people have more hairs on their head than dark-haired people.

Your belly button is the scar left from your umbilical cord. Whether it's an 'innie' or an 'outie' depends on the shape and size of your umbilical cord when you were born.

Horrified basketball fans thought they saw player Allan Ray get his eye poked out by an opponent during a game. In fact, his eyelid was stuck so far back that it only looked like his eyeball had come out of its socket. Still…ouch!

More than 62 per cent of the US population is classed as overweight or obese.

Although it is rare, some people suffer from total colour blindness and see everything in shades of grey...just like on an old TV!

You feel hot when you blush because you're blushing all over! Embarrassment triggers a rush of blood through all your blood vessels, even the ones in your stomach.

You were a single cell for the first half hour of your life.

You have more pain sensors in your skin than any other type of sensor.

More of the world's babies are born in August than in any other month.

Your nails grow more quickly as you get older.

Your nose is so sensitive that it can identify more than 10,000 different smells.

It's impossible to cry in space – the lack of gravity means that tears wouldn't trickle!

Dermatoglyphics is the study of fingerprints. It's also one of the longest words without any letter repetition in the English language!

Your nose is busy making mucus all day long, but you swallow most of it – about one cupful. Gross!

Men have more nose hair than women… and it grows longer as they get older!

The lenses in your eyes are designed to focus light in air. Water bends light so that your eyes can't focus it properly – that's why everything's blurred if you keep your eyes open underwater!

French doctor Frédéric Saldmann insists that people should burp, fart and sweat freely to reduce the risk of cancer.

It takes six hours for a coating of plaque to form after cleaning your teeth. If you don't brush it off, it eventually becomes tartar: a rock-hard substance that your dentist has to scrape off.

Your skin is your largest organ...and the only one that you need to wash!

Only humans and chimpanzees get the urge to yawn when they see another do it.

In the last minute, at least 30,000 dead skin cells came off your body. You lose about 50 million of them every day!

Your eyes produce three sorts of tears: basal tears to keep the eyes moist; reflex tears when you get something in your eyes; and psychic tears when you cry with sadness, happiness or pain.

People begin to get shorter from around 30 years of age…but only very gradually.

Japanese scientists have discovered a way of extracting a vanilla-like fragrance from manure that could be used in cosmetics. Get ready for cow dung bubble bath!

Your sense of smell is better during the day than first thing in the morning.

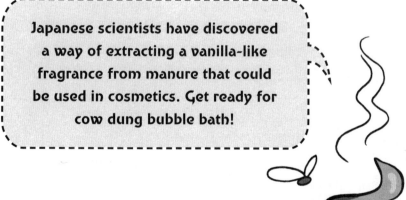

Sebum is the oily stuff secreted by glands in your skin to keep it soft. The only part of your body that doesn't have any is your lips – that's why they dry out easily.

Your saliva is made up of 98 per cent water.

About 80 hairs drop out of your head every day, but that still leaves you with more than 99,900 to play with while new ones grow!

0.2 per cent of the world's population has an extra finger or toe. That's 12 million people with an extra digit or two!

You have mucus in your eyes! It's there to make your tear fluid spread evenly.

Taste buds aren't just on your tongue – there are more than 2,000 of your them in your throat and on the roof of your mouth.

On reaching the ripe old age of 109, British pensioner Edna McLure declared that her secret was a regular snack of bread dipped in sherry.

The 250,000 sweat glands in your feet make them one of the sweatiest parts of the body. Adults produce two whole cups of that stinky foot juice every week!

If your dead skin cells didn't drop off, after three years your skin would be as thick as an elephant's!

Falling coconuts kill ten times more people than sharks do every year.

Right-handed people tend to chew food on the right side of the mouth, while left-handed people chew more on the left.

Newborn babies don't cry tears. It takes a few weeks for their lacrimal glands to start working.

You have two types of fat under your skin and around your organs: *white adipose tissue* and *brown adipose tissue*. They both keep you warm, but the brown fat gives extra insulation, so you had more of it when you were born than you do now.

A bloodhound's sense of smell is thousands of times more sensitive than that of a human.

Point to the dent between the bottom of your nose and your top lip. Now ask a friend what it's called. They won't know! You can tell them: it's your *philtrum*.

A 20-stone German man was saved by his rolls of fat when he was shot during a mugging – the bullet lodged itself in the fat and he was uninjured.

Each of your taste buds senses only one of the five basic flavours: sweet, sour, bitter, salty and the recently discovered *umami* (savoury).

A koala's fingerprints look very similar to a human's. If a crime scene smells of eucalyptus, it was definitely the koala that did it!

If you ate nothing but carrots, your skin would turn orange!

Some toiletries and make-up products contain *carmine*: a colouring made from crushed beetles!

Thick, dark hair grows more quickly than fine, fair hair.

Soap works by sticking to dirt particles so that they come away from the skin. You can see the difference by washing dirty hands with just water first!

People can choose to have their bodies deep frozen after death in case scientists come up with a way of bringing them back to life…but they will have to pay around £85,000/ US$120,000 for the privilege.

A scab isn't just a scab – your body uses 16 different chemicals to make one.

The little pink lump in the corner of your eye is what remains of an extra eyelid that our predecessors had.

Each hair on your head grows for up to six years. Then it stops, hangs around for a while and eventually drops out!

If you can curl your tongue into a tube, you're in the 85 per cent of the population who can. It's not very useful, though…

Although your ears will grow throughout your life, your hearing will just get worse. What a bad design!

Your skin is at its thinnest on your eyelids and at its thickest on the soles of your feet.

If you want muscles like Popeye, you should eat thyme – it contains ten times more iron than spinach.

Although there are 6.9 billion sets of unique human fingerprints on the planet, each has one of three basic fingerprint pattern types: arch, loop or whorl.

The largest touch sensors under your skin are called *Pacinian endings*. Seen under a microscope, they look a bit like teeny weeny squashed onions!

The hairs that you can see are dead, so it doesn't hurt when you have a haircut. They have sensors on the roots, though, so you feel them move…and you yelp if someone pulls them!

Lots of animals cry tears when they're in pain, but only humans cry tears when they are upset or happy.

Tattoos have been around for thousands of years – there were 57 on a mummified man's body discovered in the Austrian Alps, dating from 3300BC.

If you kept all your loose eyelashes and lined them up, they would stretch for around 30 metres/100 feet. Hopefully you'll find better ways to spend your retirement…

You have more than a thousand sensors in just 2.5 square centimetres/1 square inch of skin.

If you have straight hair, your hair follicles are round. If your hair is curly, it sprouts from oval follicles.

If you're right-handed, you will sweat most under your right arm. If you're left-handed, you're more likely to get a pit patch under your left arm!

Nail fungus, bacteria and viruses lurk in nail files...so it's best not to share in this case!

Women have a better sense of smell than men.

Scientists do not know why tickling is funny or why you can't tickle yourself.

Being too hot or too cold in bed increases your chances of having bad dreams.

JewelEye is a body modification procedure available from Dutch eye clinics: the eye membrane is sliced open and a decorative platinum shape is inserted. It's not available anywhere else in the world, as it's dangerous… and just crazy!

Phil Moore is one hairy Australian – he hasn't had a shave or a haircut for more than ten years!

You have hardly any taste buds in the centre of your tongue.

If you ever need stitches, they could be made from *catgut*. Don't worry – it's actually made from sheep or goat intestines. Which is sort of better…

Fingernails grow four times faster than toenails. Your fastest growing nail is the one on your middle finger.

Although identical twins have the same DNA, their fingerprints are different.

Your skin produces substances that are naturally antibacterial and antifungal. If it didn't, you would go mouldy!

One in three people will have a surgical operation in their lifetime.

Your hair grows more quickly when it has warmth and light than in the cold and dark, so you need haircuts more often in the summertime.

Sticky earwax glows in ultraviolet light.

You have more than 120 million rods and 7 million cones in your eyes! The rods help you to see in the dark, but detect only shades of grey. The cones are what let you see details and over 100,000 colours.

Women blink more than men, and adults blink more than children. Newborn babies blink only once or twice a minute!

Men need to shave so often because beard hair grows faster than any other body hair. If a man let his beard grow forever, it would reach a length of more than 9 metres (28 feet).

On average, it takes seven minutes to get to sleep.

No one in the world has the same voiceprint as you. Your larynx, nose and mouth shape all affect the way you speak, so your voice is unique.

One person in ten is left-handed.

You cannot sneeze with your eyes open.

A dead body has to be put in a fridge so it doesn't go off! Bodies in a morgue are kept at a temperature of 2–4 degrees Celcius/ 35–39 degrees Fahrenheit.

Your eye's cornea is the only part of your body that has no blood supply, since it needs to be clear for you to see through it. What it does have is lots of nerve endings – that's why a scratch in your eye is so painful.

When a Dutch gym ran naked workouts, only men turned up to the first session. Some things are better done with clothes on, no?

Over your lifetime, you will blink 415 million times.

Poisons in the body can be detected in hair, even decades after death.

Women in Japan live longer than anyone else on the planet, with a life expectancy of 86 years.

The best reason for not biting your fingernails is that there are more germs underneath them than on a toilet seat!

Identical triplets are rare: there is just one case in every 512,000 births.

Your teeth are protected by enamel, which is the hardest substance in your body.

Your funny bone isn't a bone, but the place on your elbow where a nerve crosses the bone's surface. Knocking it certainly doesn't make you laugh…

They may look different, but your hair and fingernails are made from the same stuff: *keratin*. **It's what a cow's horns and a lion's claws are made from, too!**

𝖄ou're as hairy as King Kong! People and gorillas are covered with around five million hairs; the difference is that ape hair is much thicker and longer.

Men have slower breathing rates than women and children.

Almost half of your body's heat is lost from your head, which is why you should always wear a hat on a cold day.

Your salivary glands (which produce saliva) slow right down when you're asleep, which is why you wake up with a dry mouth and stinky breath!

When your hair is wet, it's about 1.5 times longer than when it's dry.

You have around two hours' worth of dreams each night.

You will be slightly shorter tonight than you were this morning because gravity squashes your spine a little during the day. Don't worry, you won't get shorter and shorter – your spine stretches again as you lie flat in bed.

You have squidgy jelly in your eyes! Clear *vitreous humor* is what gives your eyeballs their shape.

There are millions of things living in your mouth! Don't bother looking, though – they are micro-organisms that are too small to see.

Peat bogs are very acidic and have low oxygen levels, so bodies left in them are pickled! The internal organs and facial features of bog bodies are well preserved, even if they are thousands of years old.

Each of your eyebrow hairs drops out after ten weeks.

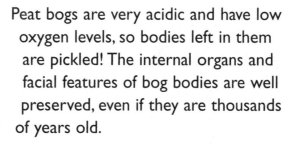

People who lose a limb or an eye can often still feel 'phantom' pains or itches in the missing part.

It's impossible for hair to turn white from shock. What can happen, though, is that a shock makes pigmented hair suddenly fall out, so someone with a mixture of coloured and grey hair would then be left with only grey hairs.

Rhinotillexomania is the scientific word for picking your nose.

Your eyes make around 4 litres/8 pints of tears a year!

More than 11.6 million cosmetic surgery procedures are carried out in the USA every year...

If you cut yourself, your blood will start clotting to form a scab in less than ten seconds.

Inside Your Insides

There are no harmful bacteria in fresh urine, so it's perfectly safe to drink. Safe? Yes. Disgusting? Absolutely!

All your muscles contract when you sneeze. Even your heart stops beating for a fraction of a second!

Your body is made up of more than 230 joints.

When you were born you had more than 300 bones, but you'll have only 206 by the time you finish growing! Don't worry, you won't lose them along the way – some of your smaller bones will just fuse together to make bigger bones.

You have several different metals in your body, such as iron in your blood and potassium in your nervous system. Calcium is what you have the most of – that's what makes your bones and teeth hard.

A caterpillar has more muscles in its body that you do!

You have three sorts of rib: true ribs are attached to your spine and breastbone; false ribs are attached to your spine and lowest true ribs; floating ribs are attached to just the spine. No spare ribs, though…

There are no toilets on the moon, so astronauts have to wear a *maximum absorption garment* when they go on spacewalks. Yep, that's a big nappy!

People who exercise too much can develop athletic heart syndrome, where the heart becomes enlarged from having to pump extra blood around the body.

Your brain is a very demanding organ – it uses one-fifth of your body's blood, oxygen and energy supplies.

Joe Stalnaker from Arizona suffers from seizures. Luckily, he has a companion who can call an ambulance when it happens – his specially trained German shepherd dog, Buddy!

If a person's liver stops working, they will die within 24 hours.

Your heart is busy every second of the day – and it beats around 35 million times a year.

You have a tailbone at the end of your spine! It is called the *coccyx* – meaning 'cuckoo' – because it looks like a cuckoo's beak.

You can control some of your muscles, but others are doing their own thing! Your *involuntary muscles* control bodily functions such as heartbeat and digestion.

Sword-swallowers train themselves to control the gag reflex that occurs when something touches the soft palate at the back of the mouth. If you touch it, you'll vomit…so don't try it!

Your brain weighs half as much as your skin.

You have stripy muscles! The ones that are joined to your bones – the skeletal muscles – are made up of light and dark coloured fibres that give a striped effect.

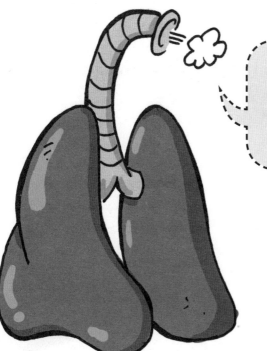

You will breathe in around 18 kilograms/40 pounds of dust over your lifetime – that's about 18 large bags of flour!

One in 600 people are born with kidneys that are fused together in a horseshoe shape.

If you took out your intestines and uncoiled them, they would be about four times as tall as you.

Being born is really stressful! As you came into the world, you had higher levels of the stress hormone *adrenaline* in your body than an adult would during a heart attack.

Only 4 per cent of your blood is in your heart right now. The rest is racing around your body!

The average person stores one million pieces of information in his or her brain.

If you eat a lot of beetroot, your urine can turn pink!

When you feel thirsty, your body is already dehydrated. It's your brain's way of telling you to get a drink, quick!

There are more cases of heart attacks on a Monday than on any other day.

The brain cannot feel pain, so some brain surgery can be done while the patient is awake! The surgeon will then talk to the patient during the operation to make sure that healthy parts of the brain are not being affected.

Babies under the age of six months automatically shut down their lungs when they are underwater.

Your bones are not as dry as you might think – they are made up of 20 per cent water.

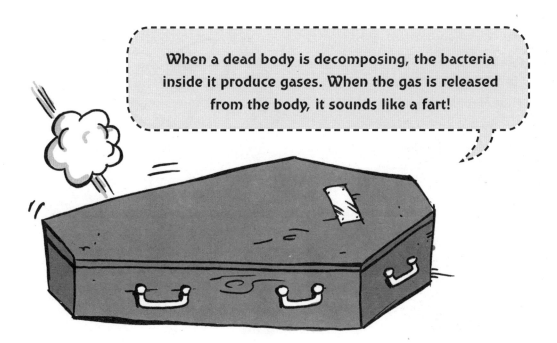

When a dead body is decomposing, the bacteria inside it produce gases. When the gas is released from the body, it sounds like a fart!

Your biggest bones are soft centred! They contain jelly-like *bone marrow*, which makes three million new blood cells every second.

If you get pins and needles, it means you've squashed a nerve or two.

When you have a bad tummy bug, you will eventually throw-up green vomit. The colour comes from bile, which is deep down in the stomach and comes up only when nothing else is left.

Your tiniest blood vessels are called *capillaries*. You have more than 10 billion and they're so narrow that red blood cells have to travel down them in single file!

Take one step forward. You just used at least 200 muscles!

More than 40,000 pints of donated blood are used each day in Canada and the USA.

Your brain helps you to digest food! A tiny part deep inside it, called the *hypothalamus*, tells you whether you're hungry and the brain stem controls the passage of food through the digestive system.

You sit on the largest muscles in your body! You have a *gluteus maximus* in each buttock.

What is wedge-shaped, dark red and spongy? Your liver!

Your lungs are not the same. The right one has three lobes (sections), while the left one has only two and is slightly smaller to make room for your heart.

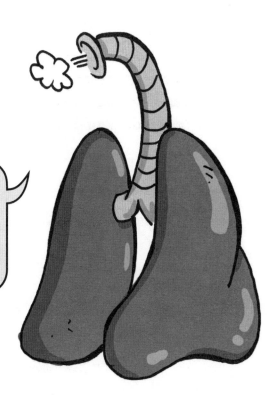

One in 20 people will have an epileptic fit in their lifetime.

Your brain is surrounded by liquid! *Cerebrospinal fluid* cushions the brain to protect it from bumps and sudden movements. It constantly needs topping up, so is being made by your body all the time.

If a muscle unexpectedly tightens up and makes you cry out in pain, you have cramp!

Your spine takes more strain when you laugh or cough than when you stand or walk. Some people have even developed back injuries from coughing.

Your bones are growing and hardening all the time. They won't stop until you're at least 20 years old!

There are more than 700 kinds of bacteria lurking in your intestine, including a harmless form of E. coli.

Make your hand into a fist – that's how big your heart is!

You have a gland in your neck that is shaped like a butterfly. The thyroid makes important substances for body development and energy production.

Almost half of the bones in your body are in your hands and feet.

There is so much electrical activity going on in your brain that you could power a light bulb with it!

What gives faeces their normal colour is *bilirubin*, a brown substance that comes from the breakdown of old blood cells in the liver.

Your brain is about 75 per cent water. That's why you should make sure you drink enough.

In the last minute, 300 million cells died in your body.

Newborn babies have no kneecaps. The triangular patella bones don't develop until after two years of age.

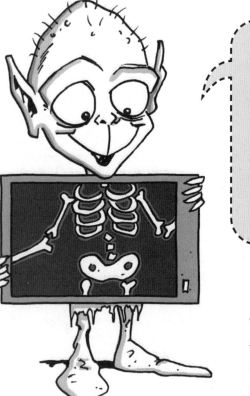

You probably have two kidneys...but you could have more. People with extra kidneys don't find out until they have a scan for other problems. British teenager Laura Moon discovered she had four kidneys altogether when she had a scan for stomach pains!

The back part of your brain deals with messages from your eyes, so badly bumping the back of your head can affect your sight.

If you could remove your brain and spread it out, it would be the size of a pillowcase.

More than 50 trillion cells make up the human body.

Your body is used to the oxygen levels around you and needs time to get used to any changes. If you go up a mountain too quickly, your body will react to the sudden drop in oxygen by throwing-up.

You do all your growing when you're asleep. So if you want to be taller, you should try getting an early night…

Muscles can only pull, not push. To move your arm in two directions, you have muscles to pull it one way…then different muscles to pull it the other way!

You have a thin, worm-like pouch hanging from your intestine: it's called your appendix!

You have an army of white blood cells to protect your body from infection. They march along your blood vessel walls, seeking out and destroying bacteria.

A really big sneeze can make you fracture a rib.

The pH level in your stomach is 1 or 2, which is more acidic than vinegar.

If you ever want to classify what you leave behind in the toilet, you should take a look at the Bristol Stool Chart. The seven types of stool listed range from 'separate hard lumps, like nuts' (Type 1) to 'entirely liquid' (Type 7).

It takes babies around six months to get used to the chilly outside world, as the temperature is at least 15 degrees Celsius/59 degrees Fahrenheit cooler than inside Mum's tum!

Zooming up and down in an aeroplane can create the weightlessness that astronauts experience in space. It's not recommended for anyone who suffers from motion sickness – those planes aren't known as 'Vomit Comets' for nothing!

It takes just 10 seconds for a person to become unconscious if blood stops flowing into the brain.

One person in 20 has an extra pair of ribs. If the extra bones cause problems, they can be removed.

It takes your kidneys just four minutes to clean all the blood in your body.

More than half of your blood is made up of *plasma*, a pale yellow fluid containing nutrients, proteins and waste products.

It's important to eat healthily, but you should ignore British chef Antony Worrall Thompson's suggestion to include *henbane* in salads – it's a poisonous weed!

Your body cannot digest tomato seeds – they pass straight through your intestines. Eat some today and see for yourself!

Around 50 tonnes of food will pass through your stomach over your lifetime.

More people die between 3am and 4am than at any other time, as this is when all the body's functions slow right down.

The smallest muscle in your body is deep inside your ear. It's joined to the smallest bone in your body, the *stirrup*.

Although your gastric juices contain powerful acids, they cannot digest chewing gum. Small amounts will get through the digestive system, but too much can cause a serious blockage…so always spit it out.

By the time each of your red blood cells dies, it has travelled around the body 250,000 times.

If you could touch your brain, it would feel like jelly!

Your bendiest muscles are the ones in your tongue!

When it is empty, your bladder is all wrinkly.

Your blood is made up of 92 per cent water.

The body's largest internal organ is the liver. It's also one of the busiest – it has more than 500 jobs to do and needs two blood supplies.

Does your tummy ever rumble or growl? The proper name for it is *borborygmus* and it's the sound of muscles contracting in your digestive system.

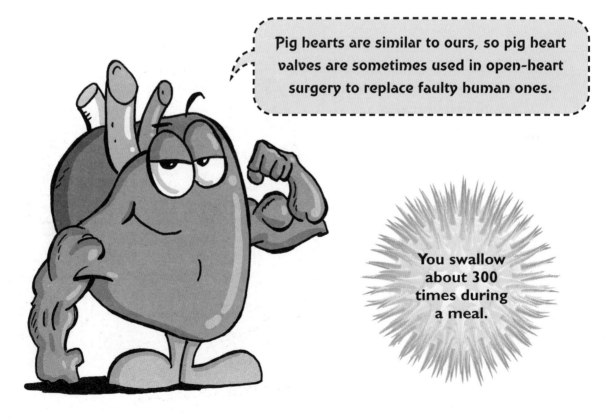

Pig hearts are similar to ours, so pig heart valves are sometimes used in open-heart surgery to replace faulty human ones.

You swallow about 300 times during a meal.

You have bendy bones! Young people's bones are not rigid, so they can bend slightly if necessary. They break only if they're bent too much, so be careful…

Your memory is super speedy – it takes you less than a second to remember something.

All those quick trips to the toilet add up to about 45,000 litres/95,000 pints of urine over a lifetime. That would fill a swimming pool!

The inside of your small intestine looks like it is covered with tiny fingers! These *villi* give your intestine the largest possible surface area for you to get the maximum amount of nutrition from your food.

You need twice as much oxygen as someone over 80 years of age.

Your gallbladder is dark green…in case you were wondering!

Despite being one of the most precious metals on the planet, gold is used in medicine! Gold salts can reduce swelling and are given by injection to treat arthritis, while gold tooth crowns are the best that you can get!

Your inner body regularly springs little leaks of blood, but the blood quickly clots to plug the hole. If it didn't clot, your insides would just keep bleeding!

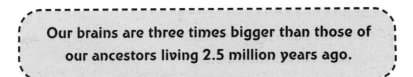

Our brains are three times bigger than those of our ancestors living 2.5 million years ago.

Each of your muscle fibres is as thin as a hair.

Your body can manage for longer without food than it can without sleep.

The longest bone in your body is your femur, or thighbone.

The thighbone of the tallest man ever was around 72 centimetres/2 feet 5 inches long!

The major blood groups – A, B, AB and O – were first identified in 1901. See if you can find out what type you are!

Vomit is a yucky cocktail of half-digested food, stomach mucus, saliva and gastric acids.

The 'butterflies' you feel when you're excited or scared are muscles tightening inside your tummy.

Most of the food you eat spends between one and three hours in your stomach, but fatty foods hang around for longer.

You have more red blood cells than any other type of cell.

You have seven neck bones, the same as a giraffe. The giraffe's bones are just longer!

Foreign bodies can occasionally get left behind during operations. Things that have been sewn inside patients include clamps, surgical sponges, scalpels, scissors, forceps and doctors. Okay, only kidding about the last one!

When you cough, air rushes through your windpipe at 100 kilometres/60 miles an hour.

Heartburn has nothing to do with the heart: it's the burning pain of stomach acid leaking back into the *oesophagus* (gullet).

Only a few hundred people in the world have the rarest blood type, which is H-H. They can't receive blood transfusions from any other blood group, so sometimes need to store their own blood before an operation.

Some of your body's muscles stretch to twice their relaxed length when you exercise.

One in five British men dies from heart disease.

You have floating bones! Your kneecaps and the horseshoe-shaped *hyoid* in your neck are not attached to any other bone.

About 1 litre/2 pints of blood passed through your liver in the last minute!

A pinhead-sized piece of your brain contains 60,000 nerve cells called neurons.

If you ever jump suddenly when you're falling sleep, you're experiencing a *hypnic jerk*. As your body relaxes, the brain mistakes the nerve messages for a falling sensation and stiffens the body to get it upright again.

When you are asleep, your heart rate is about 10 per cent lower than it is when you are awake.

If you eat asparagus, your urine will smell of rotten cabbages! The whiff comes from a gas called *methanethiol*, which is produced when you digest the vegetable.

About 0.01 per cent of the population has internal organs on the opposite side to everyone else, with no ill effects – basketball player Randy Foye has *situs inversus* and is as fit as the next man!

Nerve signals travel incredibly fast – a nerve message from your toe will reach your brain in less than one hundredth of a second.

A decapitated head can remain conscious for about 25 seconds.

You have more than 630 muscles in your body. Even if you're sitting still, lots of muscles are working to do things like make you breathe and keep your blood flowing. Reading this uses your eye muscles, too!

Two million tiny *nephrons* in your kidneys are filtering your blood as you read this!

Your liver is your body's store cupboard – it keeps iron, vitamins, minerals, sugar, proteins and emergency blood for whenever you need them.

You have slimy mucus in your stomach. It stops the acidic digestive juices burning the stomach lining and protects it from enzymes. If it didn't, you'd digest yourself!

Your blood goes on a 19,000-kilometre/12,000-mile journey every day!

Most of the functions in your body use up water, which is why you need regular drinks throughout the day.

When you're working in a maths lesson, you're using the left side of your brain.

Your heart first started beating eight months before you were born.

Donated blood is separated into red cells, white cells and plasma. That means each donation can help three people who need any one of them during surgery.

Your kidneys filter all your blood about 150 times a day.

Neurons carry nerve messages to and from your brain. The tiniest ones are smaller than a full stop, while the longest ones are 1 metre/ 3 feet long!

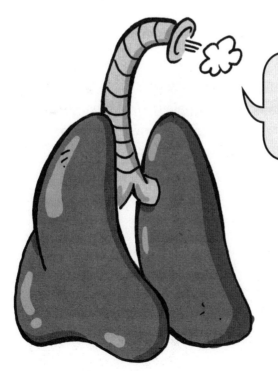

The lungs can survive after being removed from the body longer than any other organ.

You can't digest fibre, which is in fruit, vegetables and whole foods. So why bother eating it? Because it keeps your digestive system running smoothly.

A 'brain freeze' headache occurs when the cold food or drink in your mouth triggers a nerve message to the brain that says you're in a cold environment. Your blood vessels suddenly swell to warm you up...and it hurts!

It takes seven seconds for a piece of food to reach your stomach after you swallow it.

Dislocating a shoulder joint is normally painful, but some contortionists can do it by choice.

Sunburn damages your blood vessels so badly that it takes them months to repair themselves. It can also cause permanent damage, including skin cancer.

Did you know that your bones are alive? They're full of living cells, which is why they can mend themselves.

If you could look inside your bones, you would see that they're full of holes – just like a sponge! If your bones were solid, they would be too heavy to move about.

Artificial colours with names like sunset yellow (E110) might sound nice, but a recent study showed that they could damage your brain as much as fumes from leaded petrol. Lots of sweet companies use natural colours, so check the packaging on your favourites.

Emetophobia is an irrational fear of vomiting.

Every second, each nerve cell in your brain receives over 100,000 messages.

Laughing cancels out the hormones in your body that make you feel stressed, so if you have a test coming up, just laugh about it!

Modern toilets are not ideally designed for their purpose, as squatting is the best position for the body to be in when passing a stool.

Electrical activity in the brain can continue for up to 37 hours after death.

There are 250 million blood cells in a tiny drop of blood.

When you vomit, the muscles in your stomach and intestines go into reverse: instead of pushing the food down, they push it up and out of your mouth.

When used as a food additive in luxurious desserts or drinks, gold is labelled as E175. It's just there for decoration and your body doesn't digest it – so if you eat gold, you poop gold!

Unwelcome Visitors

British tourist Tanya Andrews developed a lump on her scalp after a holiday in Costa Rica. Her doctor confirmed that a botfly maggot had hatched from a mosquito bite and burrowed its way into her skin to hitch a ride back!

Head lice slurp blood from your scalp! Don't panic, they're so tiny that you won't feel a thing…

Bedbugs are the vampires of the pest world – they hate sunlight and prefer to venture out to bite you at night.

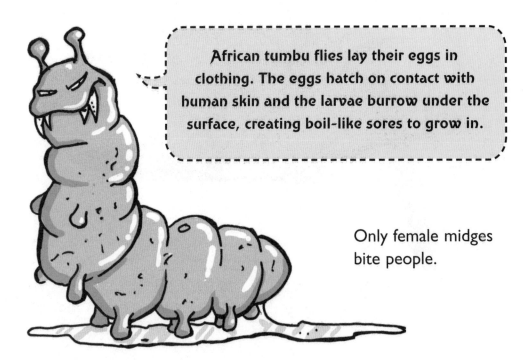

African tumbu flies lay their eggs in clothing. The eggs hatch on contact with human skin and the larvae burrow under the surface, creating boil-like sores to grow in.

Only female midges bite people.

A skunk's sulphurous spray will make your eyes sting and leave you gasping for air.

The aggressive Australasian funnel-web spider has such sharp fangs that they can pierce through fingernails and soft shoes.

Helmintophobia is a fear of getting worms. Hands up anyone who *isn't* scared!

Harvest mite larvae are tiny orange parasites that love to eat your skin. They inject digestive juices into you to make a well of liquefied skin cells that they can then suck up. They drop off when they're done, leaving behind a nasty irritation.

A long-term Argentinian study has shown that worm infestations reduce the symptoms of the illness multiple sclerosis. The health of purposely infested sufferers improved dramatically – they just had to cope with worms for years instead!

When hotel receptionist Abbie Hawkins felt something moving on her chest whilst at work, she discovered a baby bat nestled inside her bra! The bat-hiding underwear had been left on the washing line the previous night.

If a wasp stings you, it's female. Ooh, nasty girl!

At just 1 millimetre/0.04 inches long, the tropical chigoe flea is the smallest known flea. Unlike other fleas, it is rubbish at jumping.

A broad tapeworm can grow in the intestine for decades, reaching a length of 10 metres/33 feet. Worst of all, you may not even know you have one...

Mosquitoes hate the smell of garlic, so you can try eating some to keep them at bay. You can ward off vampires into the bargain, too!

When South African woman Elsie van Tonder tried to help a seal back into the sea, it bit off her nose! A helpful bystander picked up her nose, but it couldn't be reattached.

The common housefly carries more diseases than any other creature in the world.

In severe cases of worms, a large group can clump together in a ball and cause a blockage in the intestine or bowel.

Amoebic dysentery is severe diarrhoea caused by a parasite that kills around 70,000 people every year. It can travel from the intestine to the liver, where it creates pus-filled abscesses.

Demodex mites are tiny parasites that live in eyebrows and eyelashes. They're very common, especially in older people. Under a microscope, they look like worms with stubby legs.

Parasites are happily living in at least 75 per cent of the world's population.

Eye gnats love to slurp up tear fluid, so will try to hang around your eye area.

Worms eaten in raw or undercooked fish can cause bad stomach cramps. Some people can also have a severe allergic reaction to them, known as *anaphylactic shock*.

Flea eggs don't hatch unless there is a host nearby to feast on.

Many dogs and cats have worms that you can catch. If the worm infection *toxocariasis* is left untreated in a person, it can spread to their liver, brain and eyes.

Weil's disease is a serious infection that causes jaundice and kidney damage. It comes from rats' urine and is usually caught from infected water.

Black flies breed in fast-flowing rivers and spread a worm that destroys the human eyes in the tropical disease *river blindness*.

Bedbugs and fleas can live in your house for a whole year without feeding.

Raw sewage (what goes down the toilet) is often used to fertilize fields in developing countries, but it can be full of worm eggs. When the egg-infested vegetables are eaten, worm infections are spread further.

The sting from a box jellyfish is extremely toxic and fast-acting, affecting the heart and nervous system. It can kill a person within four minutes.

The tiny scabies mite tunnels along beneath the skin in a zig-zag shape, causing unbearable itching.

Girls are more likely to have head lice than boys, as they tend to have longer hair...and they do more hugging!

Don't think that you can spot head lice more easily in light hair – those critters can change colour to merge with their surroundings.

The female threadworm lays between 10,000 and 20,000 eggs at a time on its human host's bottom. She then spreads around a secretion that causes itching, to make the host scratch at the eggs and share them with friends…

The venom released by the hairs on a South American silk moth caterpillar stops blood clotting. As a result, an unlucky human victim can bleed to death.

Maggot-like parasites were found lurking in rice about to be served at a school in Suffolk in England. Who says school dinners are yucky?

Some tapeworm eggs can grow into a cyst as large as a grapefruit, filled with thousands of tapeworm heads! It's not common, so don't have nightmares…

Around 40 Americans die from allergic reactions to insect stings each year.

A spitting cobra will defend itself by shooting poison into a person's eyes to make them scream in agony and leave them temporarily blind.

Sand flies spread the parasitic disease *leishmaniasis* through their bites. The parasites cause boils on the skin, which can last for up to a year and leave bad scars. If they find their way into the body, the parasites can also damage the internal organs.

There are more than 2,500 types of mosquito worldwide, spreading viruses and parasites that kill millions of people every year.

The sting from a stonefish will paralyse you and send you into shock.

While mosquitoes puncture the skin and suck up blood, horseflies have serrated jaws that they use to bite a chunk out of your skin so they can lap up the dribble of blood.

Dead dust mites and mite droppings are a major cause of asthma.

Gnathostoma spinigerum is a worm that wriggles around under the skin and causes an itchy, snake-shaped rash during an infestation known as *creeping eruption*.

One of the most common waterborne diseases worldwide is *cryptosporidiosis*. Microscopic parasites swallowed in infected water hatch inside the intestine and cause severe diarrhoea.

Vaccines to protect against parasitic diseases are not yet available…so we'll have to live with them for a little longer!

The first insects to home in on a dead body are flies, as they like their maggots to have a moist corpse to feed on.

The wuchereria parasitic worm causes *elephantiasis*, a disfiguring disease where the limbs swell alarmingly and the skin thickens, becoming ulcerated.

We're not the only ones to be bothered by head lice – even the ancient Egyptians had to put up with them.

An ear infection can be caused by an insect that has crawled into your ear and died.

Mosquitoes spread malaria when they bite and pass on saliva containing parasites. The parasites then travel through the bloodstream and multiply in the liver and red blood cells.

Bilharzia is a flatworm infection caught by paddling or swimming in tropical lakes. It can damage the stomach, bladder and liver, so think carefully next time you're tempted to go for a swim on holiday…

Body lice are even worse than head lice! They live in clothing and cause intense itching.

The female chigoe flea lays her eggs by burrowing into human skin headfirst, leaving her back end sticking out. Over two weeks, she feeds on blood and lays 100 or so eggs, before dying and falling out.

The lasting pain from an Arizona bark scorpion's sting feels like a series of electric shocks.

Malaria kills more than one million people every year.

The Amazonian giant centipede delivers venom through its sharp claws, so if you come across one... don't touch!

The worst worm infection has to be the tropical Guinea worm disease. Between one and two years after drinking infected water, a spaghetti-like worm up to 100 centimetres/40 inches long will pop out of a blister in the foot or leg.

Minute pirate bugs have a beak-like *proboscis* (a sucking mouthpart) that they stick into the skin. Ouch!

One of the largest human flea infestations in the UK was found on a farm where more than 130 million fleas carpeted the ground!

Pretty shells can hide deadly sea snails – when touched, cone snails fire a highly poisonous harpoon so sharp that it has been known to go through wetsuits.

New York City had a bedbug epidemic in 2007, when a record 6,889 calls were made to pest control companies. The tiny brown pests infested top hotels, hospitals, cinemas and schools, as well as homes.

Some maggots love to munch away at dead flesh! This can be put to good use in the healing of wounds using 'maggot therapy', as they leave healthy flesh alone.

Each female head louse lives for a month and can lay up to 150 eggs in that time.

You have at least a million dust mites crawling around your mattress and pillow, gobbling up all your old skin cells.

A man known as Snake Manu loves a bit of 'snake flossing' – he puts slim snakes, including deadly cobras, up his nose and passes them out through his mouth.

Horseflies in West Africa spread the loa loa worm through their bites. The infection is also known as *African eye worm*, as the sufferer may feel the worms wriggling across their eyeballs. Eek!

If a venomous Gila monster lizard bites your finger, it won't let go – victims have been known to arrive at hospital with the huge reptile still attached!

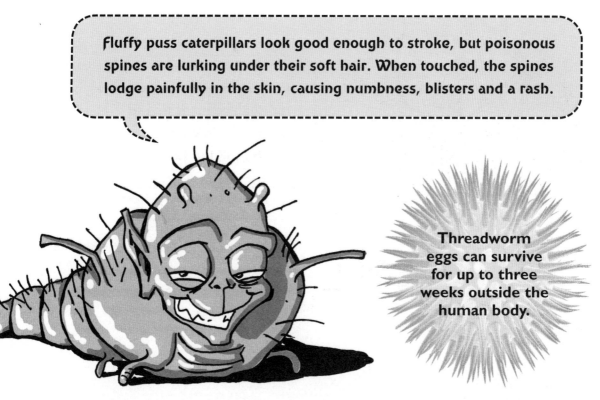

Fluffy puss caterpillars look good enough to stroke, but poisonous spines are lurking under their soft hair. When touched, the spines lodge painfully in the skin, causing numbness, blisters and a rash.

Threadworm eggs can survive for up to three weeks outside the human body.

A *zoonosis* is an infectious disease that can be transferred between animals and people, such as bird flu.

Sweat bees are so called because they love the salt in your sweat! Don't worry – their sting is almost painless compared to that of other bees.

Viper bites on limbs can be so harmful that amputation is sometimes necessary.

Someone with a bad roundworm infection will vomit worms.

It takes only two months for one pregnant flea to become an infestation of one million fleas.

The most common flea worldwide is the cat flea...which is just as happy sucking human blood, if it can't find a cat.

One type of roundworm, that can be caught by eating undercooked pork, starts off in the intestine but then wriggles off to live in the body's muscles.

A flea can live in your house for up to two years...if you don't catch it first!

The best reason to check for head lice is the saying that 'what goes in must come out'. Yep, if they're feeding on your blood, they're pooping in your hair!

Botfly eggs are spread by mosquitoes and hatch on contact with human skin. The maggots get comfy under the skin's surface and cling on with hooked spines, making them difficult to remove.

The paralysing venom of the blue ring octopus is more toxic to humans than that of any land animal.

A bite from a wheel bug causes agony that can last for up to six hours.

The largest beetle in New Zealand is the Huhu and it can give you a nasty nip with its strong jaws! It also has sharp hooks on its long legs and antennae, so its other name is the 'haircutter' – if one gets tangled in your hair, it has to be cut out with scissors!

If a woman has a worm infection, she can pass it on to her baby through her breast milk.

After 40 years of keeping bees, Michael Lynch from Derbyshire, England became allergic to bee stings.

Head lice are sensitive to heat and will abandon the head of someone with a fever.

Greedy young head lice can die from overfeeding, as their tiny guts spring a leak if they drink too much of your blood.

A jellyfish that is washed up on the shore can still sting you if its tentacles are wet.

Ticks plunge barbs into the skin of their host to keep them anchored in place. That's why they're difficult to remove!

A man who went to a Dubai hospital with a sore eye was shocked to discover that he had a 10-centimetre/ 4-inch-long worm inside it! Once removed, the parasite was identified as a canine heart worm, which doesn't normally infest humans.

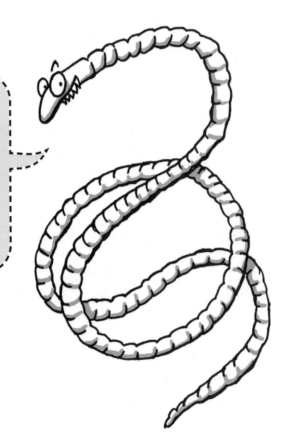

A flea that has lived on a cat with tapeworm can then pass on tapeworm eggs when it bites a human.

Leeches carry viruses, bacteria and parasites from their previous hosts and pass them on to subsequent victims.

An emerging Guinea worm makes the skin feel as if it's burning, so sufferers often soak their leg in the nearest river to soothe it. The worm then releases hundreds of thousands of larvae into the water and the cycle begins again.

A woman who went to try on some jeans in a shop in Okinawa, Japan, ended up leaving in an ambulance! She was stung by a scorpion that was hiding inside the jeans.

Mosquitoes are attracted to the carbon dioxide that you breathe out, so there's no escape!

Body lice were a huge problem for soldiers in World Wars I and II. They caused terrible itching and also spread trench fever, a disease with agonizing head, eye and leg pains that put sufferers out of action for a month.

Liver flukes are parasitic flatworms that can be caught through contaminated water or meat. They slurp blood in the liver, causing ulcers and diarrhoea.

A tick's saliva contains an anaesthetic, which is why you can't feel it biting!

Three people were stung to death by bees when a truck loaded with beehives crashed and overturned in the Jilin province of China.

Blister beetles secrete a poisonous chemical that blisters the skin on contact. The clue's in the name!

One nasty symptom of *giardiasis* is foul, sulphuric burps that can be so bad they induce vomiting! The infection is caused by a parasite that has tentacle-like limbs.

The tiny Irukandji jellyfish has a highly toxic sting that can give an unsuspecting swimmer agonizing cramps, a rapid rise in blood pressure and even a brain haemorrhage.

Head lice have little stumpy legs, so they can't jump. They don't walk very well on flat surfaces, either, so if one drops out of your hair, it is easy to catch!

More than a billion people have a hookworm infection, which means they have tiny blood-sucking worms living in their intestine. All those hookworms suck a total of 10 million litres/22 million pints of blood a day!

Biologist Mike Leahy is so committed to his work that he volunteered to swallow a tapeworm for research purposes. By the time he got rid of it, the worm was 3 metres/10 feet long!

Forensic entomologists examine the maggots and beetles on corpses to work out the time of a person's death.

A bite from a black widow spider doesn't hurt until about half an hour later; that's when the swelling, sweating, headaches and vomiting start.

Dust mites love a bit of dandruff and like to take up residence in a flaky scalp!

Stingrays have a barbed stinger on their tail, which whips up in self-defence and punctures the skin. This isn't normally fatal – Australian celebrity Steve Irwin died because the stingray's barb pierced his heart as he swam above it.

The only way to get a Guinea worm out of the skin safely is by wrapping it around a stick very…very…slowly, which can take up to a month!

Female fleas are bigger than males.

The tropical virus *chikungunya* is spread by mosquito bites and arrived in Europe for the first time in 2007. Symptoms include fever, joint pain and a severe headache.

Ticks can spread Rocky Mountain spotted fever, originally known as 'black measles'. It is a severe illness that causes fever, muscle pain, headache and a rash, and occurs all over the Americas.

There are 2,000 types of flea on the planet.

The bite of a fire ant feels like a nasty burn on your skin and turns into an itchy white blister.

1.5 billion people around the world have _ascariasis_, an infection in which earthworm-like parasites can grow as long as 30 centimetres/12 inches inside the intestine.

If you find an empty nest close to your house, ask someone to get rid of it or the hungry bird mites left behind will come inside at night to seek out your blood!

The biggest tapeworm ever found in a person's intestine was 33 metres/108 feet long. That's longer than three buses end-to-end!

Female head lice use a super-sticky protein to glue their eggs on to hair strands. You can shake your head, wash your hair or swim underwater – those eggs won't budge!

Being stung on the finger by a scorpion will send shooting pains all the way up your arm.

The Asian tiger mosquito is stripy.

Some leeches just won't let go! One Hong Kong woman had to have one surgically removed from her nostril when it clung on for weeks after she washed her face in an infested stream. The nose invader was 5 centimetres/2 inches long.

Cellulitis is a skin reaction that can follow an insect bite: the area around the bite swells alarmingly and has to be treated with antibiotics.

Forty per cent of children under the age of ten in the UK will get a threadworm infection.

Baby body lice suck blood five times a day.

Lionfish have venomous fin spines that cause agonizing stings, accompanied by nausea, breathing difficulties and convulsions.

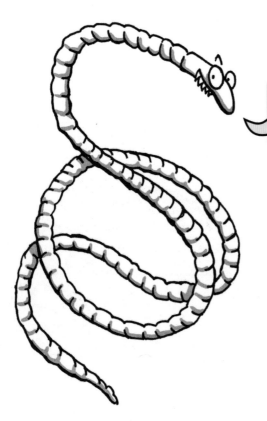

You don't have to ingest hookworms to catch them – they can bore through the skin on your feet!

In 2004, a South African man purposely released deadly puff adders into the bank that repossessed his car. A cleaner was bitten and the man was charged with attempted murder.

Threadworm eggs are so small that you can't see them. They can float through the air, so you can catch worms if the eggs zoom up your nose when you breathe in!

Head lice prefer clean hair to dirty hair, as it's easier to grip on to.

A severe bout of malaria can send a sufferer into a coma.

Some tick saliva is *neurotoxic*, which means it can affect the nervous system and cause tick paralysis.

Rat fleas spread the deadly disease *bubonic plague*. Although it's rare these days, the illness killed around one-third of the population of 14th-century Europe, when it was known as 'The Black Death'.

Hookworm larvae can penetrate the skin, causing itchy lumps that look like bites.

Intestinal myiasis means maggots in the stomach! The maggots can be swallowed in infected food and cause stomach pains, but are eventually digested by gastric juices.

Badgers may seem cuddly, but they have razor-sharp teeth and they're not afraid to use them! After a badger attacked five people in Evesham, England, one man needed plastic surgery to repair the injuries on his legs and arm.

Pediculosis is the word for being infested with lice.

Brown recluse spiders have necrotic venom, which makes a bite turn into an ulcerous sore that can be as big as 25 centimetres/10 inches across, and take months to heal.

The most painful ant bite comes from the bullet ant. Some Amazonian tribesmen purposely put them on their skin during rituals to test their bravery.

The maggots used in maggot therapy eat dead flesh, but those of the screw-worm fly eat healthy flesh. If they infest a wound, they burrow in and destroy the healthy tissue around it, making the wound far worse.

Parts of the pufferfish are poisonous enough to kill an adult human. Only specially trained chefs are able to prepare it for cooking.

A bad infestation of threadworm can cause appendicitis.

Head lice eggs are brown, but turn white once hatched.

The Congo floor maggot sucks human blood! It comes out at night looking for people sleeping on the ground.

Forty million Americans have threadworm at any one time.

Pitohui birds have a sting in their tail! Their brightly coloured feathers release a toxin, so touching them will make your fingers tingly and numb.

Leeches secrete an enzyme that stops blood from clotting as they feed. They usually drop off once they're full, but the bite carries on bleeding until the substance has been washed away.

It takes 20 minutes for a leech to fill itself up with human blood.

In large numbers, hookworms can suck so much blood from the small intestine that they can cause anaemia (iron deficiency).

St. Louis barber, Bill Black, saved the hair clippings swept from his floor and used them to make vests, shirts, ties and even a bikini! Itchy!

After five days of having his arm trapped under a fallen boulder, US mountaineer Aron Ralston had to take drastic action: he cut off his arm with a penknife.

During an argument about a fence, British pensioner June Iddon whacked her neighbour with a spade and broke his arm.

Following his arrest for drink driving, US man José Cruz was also charged with assault when he farted on a police officer. In his statement, the officer complained that 'the gas was very odorous'.

Australian performance artist Stelarc had a human ear grafted on to his forearm in the name of art. He can literally turn a deaf ear to anyone who annoys him!

When Indian man Dharmendra Singh smokes a cigarette, the smoke comes out of his ears.

Australian doctor Barry Marshall insisted that stomach ulcers were not caused by stress or spicy foods but by the bacterium *Helicobacter pylori*. He proved his point by swallowing a Petri dish full of it!

A Chinese farmer was rendered unconscious for 11 hours after catching his finger on a needle filled with anaesthetic meant for a deer.

Norwegian footballer Svein Grondalen had to miss an international match through injury after crashing into a moose whilst out jogging. Those beasts are difficult to spot...

One of singer Screamin' Jay Hawkins' songs was called 'Constipation Blues'.

British entertainer Mr Methane describes himself as 'the world's only full-time performing flatulist'. Yep, people pay to hear him fart tunes!

A Croatian pensioner was so short-sighted that he collected the wrong boy when he went to get his grandson from nursery, sparking a police manhunt.

Some cultures have a tradition of earlobe stretching: people wear heavy earrings that can weigh up to half a kilogram/1 pound and hang them from huge holes in their earlobes.

Reclusive billionaire Howard Hughes had such a phobia of germs that his staff had to cover his cutlery handles with layers of tissue paper and cellophane.

When Italian police investigated complaints against dentist-from-hell Alvaro Perez, they discovered he had been using a regular power drill on his patients and had no dental qualifications.

Some African cultures practise *scarification*, when patterns of raised scars are made on the skin as decoration or to show bravery.

A Polish car thief who left his false teeth at the crime scene was caught when police matched them to his dental records.

Fast food addicts Tom and Kerry Watts celebrated their marriage with a giant burger that contained the equivalent of 100 quarter pounders!

US man Kevin Kearney went out kite-surfing in gale force winds and was swept up from a Florida beach, receiving multiple injuries when he was smashed into a street some distance away.

Body modification fan Erl Van Aken has a flap of skin on his stomach formed into a kind of handle shape that he can put his finger through. Why? Just because!

After American cyclist Robert Evans was hit by a car in a hit-and-run accident, he was hit by a train on his way home from the hospital. What a bad day...

A Chinese man had to take his girlfriend to hospital when she swallowed the engagement ring he had hidden in her cake.

A one-month-old baby was rushed to hospital after his grandmother misunderstood instructions and sent him through the hand luggage X-ray machine at Los Angeles airport.

American performance artist 'The Lizardman' has a forked tongue, green-inked lips, sharpened teeth and green scales tattooed on his body.

Carpenter Patrick Lawler suffered blurred vision and toothache after his nail gun backfired and a nail struck his face. An X-ray six days later showed a second 10-centimetre/4-inch nail embedded in his brain!

German fishermen got a shocking catch from the River Rhine – a severed arm! Police thought it belonged to a man 'due to its hairiness'.

Dutch artist Joanneke Meester made a tiny pistol from a piece of her own skin to protest against rising levels of violence.

When two US ice hockey players collided at a match, the skate of one accidentally sliced the jugular vein of the goalkeeper. The sight of blood gushing across the ice made three spectators have heart attacks. The goalkeeper didn't feel too good either!

Olympic hurdler Peter Hildreth kept himself fit into old age – at the age of 80, he was banned from running up the down escalator in his local department store!

Zombies really do exist! Haitian witch doctors called *bokors* can use plant-based drugs to make a person appear to be dead, then revive them and keep them under their control.

Estonians have an age-old saying: if you point at a rainbow, your finger will fall off.

Hawaiian Kala Kaiwi has used wooden discs to stretch the holes in his earlobes to an eye-watering 10 centimetres/ 4 inches across.

Firefighters had to cut free a woman in Somerset, England, when she got her arm stuck in a tumble dryer whilst trying to remove the fluff from it.

The annual Mooning Amtrak event involves thousands of people showing their bottoms to passing trains in California. The organizers especially welcome decorated and obese butts!

When American recluse Homer Collyer died, police and workmen cleared rubbish from his junk-filled house for two weeks before they found the body of his brother, Langley Collyer.

A Swiss thief whose finger was cut off by broken glass was caught when police found the finger at the crime scene and matched its print with their records.

British man Richard Ross was holding a nail between his lips whilst doing DIY, when he inhaled it! His ribs had to be broken for the subsequent lung surgery to remove it.

When a five-year-old Chinese boy underwent an operation to correct a limp, the surgeons lengthened the wrong leg! The confusion arose when the boy was on his back for the anaesthetic but on his stomach for the surgery.

Several people have been injured or drowned trying to go over the edge of Niagara Falls. (And it's illegal, anyway.)

British footballer Darius Vassell tried his own treatment for a blood blister under his toenail – he drilled a hole in it! He lost half the toenail in the infection that followed.

Romanian villagers re-elected Neculai Ivascu as their mayor…even though he died just before the election.

The Si La people of Laos have an old tradition of painting their teeth: men have red teeth and women have black.

Australian rugby player Jamie Ainscough suffered a severe arm infection that puzzled doctors. The mystery was solved when an X-ray revealed an opponent's tooth embedded under his skin!

New Zealand man William Singalargh was arrested for using a hedgehog as an offensive weapon – he threw it at a youth, causing scratches and puncture wounds.

When javelin thrower Tero Pitkamaki slipped in his run-up during a competition in Rome, his javelin flew off into French long jumper Salim Sdiri, damaging his liver and right kidney.

British angler Peter Hodge wanted to be fed to the fish when he died, so his ashes were mixed with fish food and thrown into his favourite river.

After Czech President Vaclav Claus had a hip replacement operation, a police investigation began – when his original hip was put up for sale on an internet auction site!

Just some of the items awaiting collection at Transport For London's Lost Property Office include false teeth, breast implants, false limbs and a bag containing two human skulls.

US man Don Gorske has scoffed 23,000 Big Macs in 36 years. He even has the receipts to prove it!

British painter and decorator Nick Male became inundated with jobs when he offered a new service: working naked!

Having scored the winning goal against Ecuador in a 2006 World Cup match, England captain David Beckham threw-up on the pitch.

Singer Bantcho Bantchevsky jumped off a theatre balcony and killed himself during the interval of an opera at New York's Metropolitan Opera House.

Premier League footballer Leroy Lita stretched his leg on waking up one morning…and damaged a muscle so badly that he couldn't play for a month.

When a New Zealand tree surgeon with a broken leg was rescued from the top of a 40-metre/130-foot-high tree, the rescue helicopter smashed him into another tree, injuring him further!

Scientists have found a way to grow teeth! So far, only parts of a tooth have been grown from stem cells, but farmed teeth could replace false ones in the future.

British grandmother Rosie Swale Pope has more stamina than most — in her five-year charity run round the world she covered 32,000 kilometres/20,000 miles across 12 countries.

Chinese man Li Jianping has grown his fingernails for more than 15 years…but only on his left hand! Their total length is more than 1 metre/3 feet, so he avoids crowded places in case he breaks one.

England cricketer Ian Greig went for an X-ray when he injured his hand during a match…and cut his head open on the machine as he stood up, needing stitches!

One million people each decade are killed in natural disasters.

US politician Stan Jones drank a home-made silver solution in the belief that it would boost his immune system. He feels great, but his skin turned permanently grey!

US man George Chandler narrowly avoided serious brain damage when the nail gun he was using went off accidentally and nailed his hat to his head. The nail pierced his brain but was safely removed.

Pilgrims to the Tirupati temple in India give their hair as a sacrifice. The temple's 600 barbers shave thousands of visitors every day, taking 6.5 million hairy gifts every year.

A man who was diving for golf balls in a Florida lake had his arm broken by an attacking alligator. He was saved from death by a nearby golfer, who whacked the alligator with his club.

Three military band members were injured when a skydiver crashed into them at around 80 kilometres/50 miles per hour during a ceremony in Kansas, USA.

Entertainer Roy Horn was seriously injured when a tiger he used in his act gripped him in its teeth and ran off with him.

Women of the Ethiopian Surma tribe have an old tradition of putting a clay disk in the bottom lip to stretch it outwards. The lower teeth have to be removed first, though...

A World War II veteran who had been blind for 64 years had his sight miraculously restored when he was head-butted by a horse!

The US has three body farms — research centres where dead bodies are left to decay in various situations, even in the boot of a car! Scientists study the decomposition process, using the information to help with murder investigations.

Your farts could be put to good use! Inventors Michael Zanakis and Philip Femano thought so – they patented a fart-powered toy rocket in 2005.

Australian surfer John Morgan was towed 51 metres/170 feet through the ocean by a shark when it got tangled in his leg rope.

When grumpy Manchester United manager Alex Ferguson kicked a stray football boot after his team lost a match, it slammed straight into David Beckham's head and the star player needed stitches for the cut.

Yvonne's Hair and Nail Salon in Virginia is offering fish pedicures: just dip your feet in the water full of garra rufa fish and they nibble away all the flaky skin!

People travel from all over the world to enter the annual tongue-tingling Nettle Eating Championships in Dorset, England.

Chinese man Ru Anting can write on paper with water squirted from his eyes! He decided to hone his eye-spraying skill for entertainment when he lost his factory job.

Brazilian priest Adelir de Carli attached himself to 1,000 helium-filled balloons in a publicity stunt that went tragically wrong. He was blown out to sea and only the lower half of his body was found several weeks later.

British reptile shop employee Lee Thompson almost died after he was bitten by an adder in his shop...but made a full recovery and decided to keep the venomous snake as a pet!

Scientists have worked out that you have a 300 million to one chance of dying from a shark attack.

A man was banned from a pub in Scotland…because he kept doing smelly farts!

An Indian man was so desperate to go to the 2007 Cricket World Cup in the West Indies that he sold one of his kidneys to pay for the trip.

The highlight of the year in the Japanese city of Shibukawa is the Belly Button Festival. People dance in the streets with faces painted on their stomachs.

When British man John Stirling accidentally sawed off his arm with a chainsaw, he calmly asked his neighbour to help and sat on a stool till the ambulance arrived! Meanwhile, the neighbour packed the arm in a bag of frozen pastries so that it could be reattached.

Artist Marco Evaristti held a dinner party and served meatballs made with his own liposuction fat!

Football maestro Mr Woo can juggle a football with his feet – and his head, shoulders, chest and knees!

Two dopey pilots were sacked from a Hawaiian airline after falling asleep during their landing procedure. They missed their stop at Hilo Airport and had to turn the plane round to land when they woke up!

Austrian hunter Hans Biedermeier accidentally shot himself as he was shaking the snow out of his rifle during a hunting trip.

A patient in a Belgrade hospital was alarmed to discover that two surgeons had started a fight during his operation! They took their punch-up outside and the assistant surgeon completed the procedure instead.

An 80-year-old Chinese man agreed to have his hair and beard washed for the first time in 23 years. Twelve relatives and friends spent five hours getting all the grime out of his 2-metre/ 6-foot-long matted locks and 1.5 metre/5-foot-long beard!

Argentinian artist Nicola Constantino used fat removed from her body to make 100 soaps and two sculptures.

One-legged British man David Huckvale couldn't afford the computer-controlled limb that he dreamed of. However, his luck changed when a US specialist spotted him in a pub and offered him the spare one he had in his surgery…for nothing!

A Bosnian man was furious when he faked his own death to see who would attend his funeral…and only his mother turned up!

Chinese man Zhang Yinming can snort milk up his nose and squirt it out of his eyes up to 2 metres/6 feet away.

Himalayan Apatani tribeswomen used to enlarge their nostrils with 2.5-centimetre/1-inch-wide circular nose plugs.

When German man Udo Ried dropped a kitchen knife on his foot and chopped off a toe, his cat Fritz ran off with it as he hopped around phoning for an ambulance!

On reaching the top of Mount Everest, Lakpa Tharke Sherpa took all his clothes off, braving sub-zero temperatures for three whole minutes. Brrrr!

Body piercing fans like to stick jewellery in their nipples, on the back of their necks and in the soft bit between the eyes. Can you feel a bit of skin between your top gum and lip? That can be pierced, too! (And stop now, you look like a monkey.)

England cricketer Chris Lewis shaved his head on arrival in the West Indies and then played the match without a hat, giving himself severe sunstroke.

Police in Soweto, South Africa, had to deal with a series of assaults...by giant rats! The oversized rodents were nesting in old cars and attacking passers-by.

Indian artist Shihan Hussaini painted 56 portraits of politician Jayalalitha for her 56th birthday. As a personal touch, he used over a litre/2 pints of his own blood as the paint.

Hefty German bank robber Sandra Meiser tried to hold up the same branch twice. She was caught the second time when a witness recognized her huge bottom!

American playwright Tennessee Williams choked to death on a bottle top.

One way to pass the time in some parts of Africa is to take part in some kudu dung spitting. The sport involves spitting pellets of antelope dung as far as you can!

Native American body modification fan 'Stalking Cat' has tiger-stripe body tattoos, surgically elongated ears and facial implants so that he can wear whiskers.

After accidentally swallowing a toothbrush, an Indian man endured a whole week of agonizing stomach pains before finally seeing a doctor.

Italians wanting comfort beyond the grave bought tickets for a raffle with a first prize of a luxury coffin, complete with deluxe pillow and brass reading light!

For his 'Only You' exhibition, Uruguayan artist Carlos Capelán created collages made from his toenail clippings.

US celebrity Jocelyn Wildenstein has spent around US$4 million/£2.8 million on cosmetic surgery to look more 'feline'…but she just looks scary!

In the USA, more than 150 pairs of identical twins are married to identical twins.

A streaker leaped over a fence on to the pitch at an Australian football match…and managed to knock himself out when he landed!

A 1956 Olympic water polo match between Hungary and the USSR had to be abandoned when the teams had a mass punch-up.

Staff at an acupuncture clinic locked up and went home when there was still someone in a treatment room! The woman had to remove the needles herself and call for help.

A Mexican man put hooks through his upper body and used them to dangle himself from a tree to protest against the discrimination of people with tattoos and piercings.

Baseball player Glenallen Hill missed a match after having a nightmare that a spider was attacking him – he fled his bed, cutting his foot on a glass table, and fell down the stairs!

At the age of 15, British girl Jean Burgess decided that she would never have her hair cut again. When she reached 55, her hair was 1.65 metres/5 feet 6 inches long and took more than two hours to comb!

A British pensioner had to take her dog to the vet when she realized it had eaten her false teeth! The dog had a three-hour operation to have them removed. A quick rinse and they were as good as new…

Police had to guard a Bangladesh hospital after 15,000 people tried to get inside to see the two-headed baby that had been born there in August 2008.

Austrian man Harold Stein was injured in a car accident when he sat on a plastic box whilst driving. He'd taken the car seat out to clean and thought the box would be fine, but he couldn't reach the brake pedal and crashed into another car!

When a Polish man criticized the country's president, Lech Kaczynski, during a police check, he was asked to show more respect. He replied with a loud fart and was promptly arrested!

American sideshow performer Enigma has had surgery to give him horns on his head. He has a jigsaw puzzle tattoo that covers his whole body, too.

It takes just 60 seconds for Indian man Vijayakanth to pass a nylon thread through his tear duct and out through his mouth.

British performance artist Mark McGowan strapped his raised arm to a lamp-post for two weeks, draining the blood from his arm and possibly causing muscle damage. He called his anti-war protest 'The Withered Arm'.

A US company has marketed Subtle Butt – fabric strips that stick inside your underwear to neutralise farty smells. If only they were soundproof, too!

Hindus who attend the Malaysian Thaipusam festival stick skewers through their skin as part of the celebrations.

When a US man had his glasses broken and eye bruised by a snowball, he sued the thrower for more than US$4,000/£2,800.

Puerto Rican man Angel Medina's final wish was to stay standing for his three-day wake. His corpse was embalmed in an upright position and topped off with a Yankees baseball cap for relatives to say their last goodbyes.

Australian Graham Barker has 24 years' worth of his belly button fluff saved in storage jars...sorted into its different colours, of course.

Italian artist Piero Manzoni filled 90 small tins with his own faeces for a 1961 exhibition. They were sold to art buyers at a price equal to their weight in gold!

London man Herbert Crossman hung himself upside down from a crane for two hours to protest against the rising cost of living.

Nine years after being blinded in an accident, a British man got his sight back when he was struck by lightning.

A man died in Devon, England, when he stepped backwards off a cliff whilst flying a kite in 2006.

After scoring a goal, Newcastle striker Obafemi Martins does a series of back flips. Roma captain Francesco Totti celebrates a little more quietly – he sucks his thumb.

In 2002, Anatomist Gunther von Hagens carried out the first public autopsy for 170 years. Over 500 people paid to watch him slice and saw a man's body, before removing its internal organs.

A Chinese man woke up after a night out to find his prankster friends had put a heavy-duty bicycle lock round his neck! He had to ask local firefighters to cut him out of it.

Adelaide Zoo in Australia was criticized for its Orang-utan Week offer of free entry to all 'rangas' – people with ginger hair.

Brazilian-born Elaine Davidson is the world's most pierced woman. She has more than 5,000 piercings and can put her little finger through a hole in her tongue.

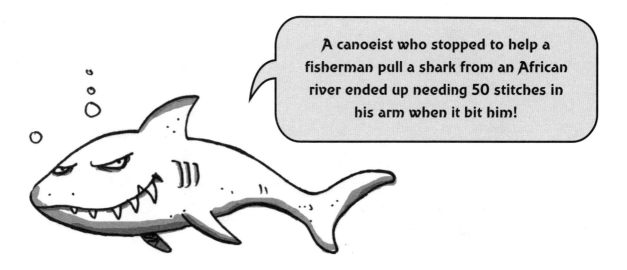

A canoeist who stopped to help a fisherman pull a shark from an African river ended up needing 50 stitches in his arm when it bit him!

New Zealand cricketer Trevor Franklin was out of action for 18 months after he was run over by a motorized luggage trolley in an airport, fracturing his leg in several places.

An unmarried Chinese man advertised for someone to share his grave so he wouldn't be lonely in the afterlife.

In 2007, Manual Uribe was officially the world's fattest man. Then he found love and lost more than 230 kilograms/560 pounds for his wedding!

Thai Karen tribeswomen traditionally wear several neck rings to lengthen their necks. The first bands are added at the age of five and more are added every few months.

A German zookeeper was almost eaten by a python whose enclosure she was cleaning out. The huge snake had her head in its mouth when it was hosed away by other staff.

British teenager Ianthe Fullagar screamed so loudly when she found out she'd won millions on the lottery that her alarmed dog jumped up and bit her on the behind!

British footballer Darren Barnard tore a knee ligament when he slipped on a puddle of his puppy's pee in his kitchen.

When a woman died in the economy section of an aeroplane shortly after take-off, she was moved to first class for the remainder of the long flight. Surely there are better ways of getting an upgrade…

Pickled human organs were found amongst the 103 tonnes/101 tons of junk removed from the Collyer brothers' house in Harlem, USA.

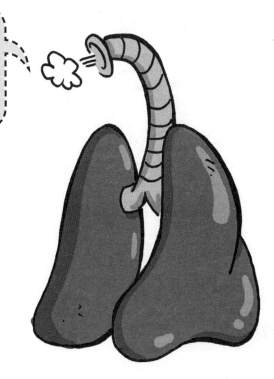

US man Matt Gone hated his birthmarks so much that he had his body covered in a checkerboard pattern to hide them. That's 500 hours' worth of tattoos!

British hypnotist Bernadine Coady hypnotized herself so that she could have an operation on her knee without any anaesthetic.

In 1900, Austrian man Johann Hurlinger walked from Paris to Vienna…on his hands!

English artist Marc Quinn made a model of his head from 4 litres/8 pints of his own deep-frozen blood. The blood for the work, entitled *Self*, was collected over five months.

Several people have donated their bodies to anatomist Gunther von Hagens so that he can *plastinate* (preserve and dissect) them for his Body Worlds exhibitions.

Canadian skater Jessica Dube needed plastic surgery after her partner's skate sliced her face during a side-by-side spin in a competition routine.

The Good
Old Days

French medical student Ernest Duchesne discovered the bacteria-destroying properties of certain moulds after seeing that mouldy saddles cured sores on horses. This was 30 years before Alexander Fleming took all the glory!

Ancient Egyptians cleaned their teeth with powder made from crushed ox hooves and burnt eggshells.

Smallpox killed 400,000 Europeans every year in the 18th century.

Ancient Greek ruler Histiaeus found a novel way of getting a secret message to his son-in-law – he tattooed it on a slave's shaven head and waited for the hair to grow back before sending him off.

Being crushed by an elephant was a common form of execution in ancient Asia.

An 18th-century Russian peasant woman gave birth to 69 children. Ooh, think of all that washing!

Bobby Leach was the first man to go over Niagara Falls in a barrel, surviving his multiple injuries. He went out with less of a fanfare, dying from gangrene after slipping on some orange peel.

A popular Victorian beauty treatment contained arsenic, vinegar and chalk. What's a little arsenic poisoning if you have perfect skin?

One of the most sought-after jobs in a medieval royal household was Groom of the Stool. Wiping the king's bottom was included in the job description!

In ancient Greece, a sneeze was believed to be a good sign from the gods.

Pliny the Elder, an ancient Roman, said eating lion fat was a cure for epilepsy. If there were no lions around, sufferers could always try one of his other suggestions – dried camel's brain in vinegar!

Ancient Egyptian physicians used acacia thorns as needles when they stitched up wounds.

Nine people died in the 1814 London beer flood, when thousands of gallons of beer gushed through the streets from ruptured brewery vats.

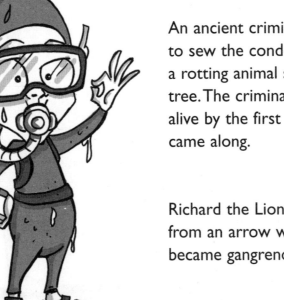

An ancient criminal punishment was to sew the condemned person inside a rotting animal skin and tie it to a tree. The criminal would then be eaten alive by the first hungry creature that came along.

Richard the Lionheart died from an arrow wound that became gangrenous.

Arctic explorer John Hornby tried to spend a year without food supplies by the Thelon River, in Canada, certain that he could live off the land. He starved to death after only a few months.

In World War I, soldiers used lumps of sphagnum moss as dressings for their wounds. It can soak up four times as much blood as cotton bandages.

French Admiral Gaspard de Coligny found a novel use for his bushy beard – he kept his toothpicks in it!

Nineteenth-century English footballer Joe Powell got *tetanus* and blood poisoning after badly breaking his arm in a match. His arm was amputated, but he died a week later.

One medieval treatment for a skin infection was to rub cow dung on it.

Greek philosopher Aristotle believed that nose mucous came from the brain.

US trainee doctor Stubbins Firth was so convinced that *yellow fever* wasn't infectious that he drank a sufferer's 'fresh black vomit'. He escaped the deadly disease even though it is contagious (but transmitted through blood).

The Native American Mandan tribe used to keep the skulls of their dead, arranging them in a circle formation near their village.

Eighteenth-century toothpaste recipes included burnt bread and dragon's blood. It's not quite as gruesome as it sounds – dragon's blood was a red plant resin.

The dentures of US President George Washington were made from hippopotamus' teeth.

Neil Armstrong, the first man on the moon, was travel sick as a child.

It was against ancient Roman law to dissect human bodies; physicians of the time had to make do with dead pigs and monkeys for their research.

Medieval soldiers used a trebuchet to catapult things over castle walls at their enemies – including severed heads!

British Prime Minister William Gladstone lost his left forefinger in an accident while reloading a gun.

Greedy Swedish monarch King Adolf Frederick's biggest meal consisted of lobster, caviar, kippers and cabbage, followed by 14 servings of his favourite dessert. It was to be his last – he died shortly afterwards of digestion problems.

The terrifying 15th-century warrior Pier Gerlofs Donia was known for his ability to chop off several enemies' heads with one swing of his great sword.

An early *typhus* vaccine was made from squished body lice infected with the deadly disease!

Immediately after declaring on a TV show that he'd never felt better in his life, US author Jerome Irving Rodale died of a heart attack.

Pakistan is the home of dentistry – 9,000-year-old skeletons discovered there had drilled and capped teeth.

Jimmy Carter was the first US President to be born in a hospital.

People living in Pompeii were trapped under deep volcanic ash when Mount Vesuvius erupted in AD79. When the bodies decomposed, they left their shapes behind in the ash and plaster casts of them were made 2,000 years later.

The *influenza* pandemic of 1918 came to be known as 'Spanish flu', even though it started in America.

Franz 'The Flying Tailor' Reichelt designed a huge overcoat that doubled as a parachute. He demonstrated his invention in 1912 by jumping off the first deck of the Eiffel Tower, but it didn't work and he died in the fall.

Obesity was frowned upon in ancient Rome. One account of the time tells of a large man having a breast reduction operation, as 'they looked unsightly and shameful'.

Dutch artist Vincent van Gogh tried to kill himself with a bullet to the chest…and took two days to die.

The 17th-century Italian lady's poison of choice was Acqua Toffana: a lethal cocktail of arsenic, lead and belladonna (deadly nightshade). Perfect for using on an annoying husband!

When 18th-century German scientist Georg Richmann rushed out to observe lightning, he was fatally struck and his shoes exploded.

Ancient Egyptian medical documents give information on how to treat burns, pus-filled abscesses, broken bones and even crocodile bites.

English commander Lord Uxbridge had to have his leg amputated after it was shattered by cannon shot at the Battle of Waterloo. It was buried in a nearby garden and became a macabre tourist attraction.

Medieval suits of armour could be a danger in themselves – many knights fighting in hot countries baked to death inside them.

In the Middle Ages, juggling was believed to be a form of witchcraft.

'Elephant Man' Joseph Merrick suffered from a severe form of the rare condition *Proteus syndrome*, which causes disfiguring skin and bone growths.

Austrian Hans Steininger should have trimmed his beard – it was so long that it tripped him up and he perished in the fire he was fleeing in 1567.

The first American toothpaste boxes were black and featured an X-ray picture of a decayed tooth. Packaging is a little more cheerful these days…

The 5th-century *smallpox* epidemic in India was believed by many to be a punishment from a god.

The body of Alexander the Great was embalmed in gallons of honey.

Ancient Roman physician Galen was a pioneer of cataract surgery, using long needles on sufferers' eyes. This was in the days before anaesthetics!

One punishment for Indian criminals in ancient times was to have their noses cut off. It was a good opportunity for surgeons of the era to practise early nose jobs!

Gerald Ford was the longest-living US president, living to the age of 93 years and 165 days.

The first US astronaut, Alan Shepard, got that warm feeling when his Mercury capsule flight was delayed for several hours – he had to pee in his spacesuit.

Infamous 19th-century serial killer Mary Ann Cotton used arsenic to fatally poison up to 20 people, including her own husbands and children. Not the family type, then…

Zeppo, the least famous of the comic Marx brothers, invented a wristwatch that sounded an alarm if the wearer was having a heart attack.

Fifteenth-century Romanian ruler Mircea II was blinded with hot stakes and buried alive by his enemies.

Medieval wart sufferers used to rub their ugly growths with a piece of raw meat and then bury it. They believed that as the meat rotted away, the warts would disappear. Warts go by themselves anyway, so that's why everyone thought it worked!

Chinese leader Mao Tse Tung had green teeth, as he never brushed them. His reasoning was that tigers never brushed theirs…

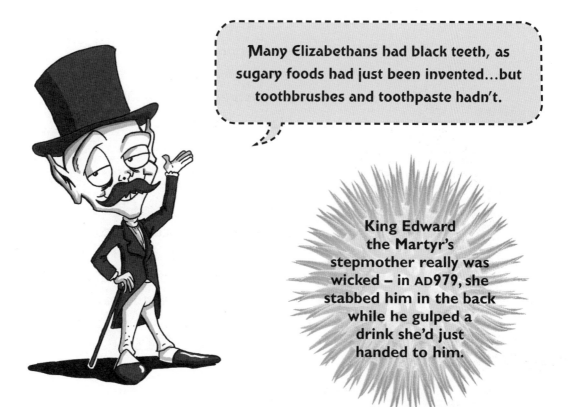

Many Elizabethans had black teeth, as sugary foods had just been invented…but toothbrushes and toothpaste hadn't.

King Edward the Martyr's stepmother really was wicked – in AD979, she stabbed him in the back while he gulped a drink she'd just handed to him.

Victims of the 1918 flu pandemic had such bad lung damage that their faces turned a blue-purple colour and they coughed up blood.

Some surgeons in ancient times tried using pigskin for nose reconstructions on people. When the skin shrivelled up and dropped off, they believed it was because the pig had died!

Vikings had no toilet paper, so they used bits of sheep's wool instead.

The medieval long sword was so big that it had to be held in both hands. It could chop off a limb, even through armour!

When Queen Elizabeth I died, it was discovered that her coronation ring was embedded in her flesh. The ring had to be sawn off before it could be passed to the heir to the throne, James VI of Scotland.

Elizabethan women used face packs made from toxic mercury to keep their skin soft.

After French artist Henri de Toulouse-Lautrec broke his legs in his early teens, they stopped growing. As an adult, he had a fully grown torso and child-sized legs.

Alexander the Great put saffron in his bath to help heal his battle wounds. He felt better afterwards – even though he was bright yellow!

If they were feeling really bloodthirsty, Vikings would kill enemies using the 'blood eagle' – the victim's ribs would be cut and opened out, then the lungs would be removed. Bad Vikings!

People suffering from warts used to pay a wart-charmer to get rid of them.

The Sultan of Istanbul had Vlad the Impaler's decapitated head preserved in honey and put on display as proof of his death in 1476.

Roller skate inventor Jean-Joseph Merlin was severely injured when he wore his skates to a ball and crashed into a large mirror.

US dancer Isadora Duncan's love for floaty scarves was to be her downfall — she was killed when the scarf she was wearing got tangled in the wheel of her car and strangled her.

After losing a battle in AD865, Viking warlord Ragnar Lodbrok was thrown into a pit of venomous snakes and was bitten to death.

Battle scars on a man's back were considered highly shameful in ancient Rome, as it suggested the soldier had turned his back on a battle.

It was believed in the Middle Ages that if you had some of your enemy's hair, you had control over him.

Workers in the 19th-century match industry often suffered from *phossy jaw* – poisonous fumes from the phosphorus used in matches rotted away their jawbones.

Whiskey distillery founder Jack Daniel kicked his safe in a temper when he couldn't open it and died from the resulting toe infection. It's said that if he'd dipped the yucky toe in some of his own whiskey, he would have been fine!

Arrow extractors were an essential part of an ancient Roman doctor's tool kit.

Spanish artist Salvador Dalí would spend longer than most in the toilet – he liked to study his stools and make notes on their colour and consistency.

When the French ship *Medusa* ran aground in 1816, those who escaped on a raft resorted to cannibalism after four days adrift.

Ancient Persians executed criminals by smothering them with honey and tying them to a boat. They would then moor it on some stinky water and leave the criminals to be eaten alive by insects.

Greek physicians were first permitted to dissect bodies around 2,000 years ago. They were also allowed to perform vivisection (the cutting up of live bodies) on criminals.

When Soviet leader Vladimir Lenin was shot in an assassination attempt, the bullet in his neck could not be removed – it stayed there until he died six years later.

Ancient Romans used to clean their teeth with urine. Mmm, refreshing!

Victorians made keepsakes such as pictures and jewellery from the hair of their deceased loved ones.

Some ancient African tribes used animal dung to stiffen their hair. No point in washing it first, then!

Allan Pinkerton, the founder of the first US detective agency, slipped in a Chicago street and bit his tongue. He didn't seek treatment and died of the infection that followed.

Catherine of Aragon had a black heart! This led to suspicions that she had been murdered, but today's scientists believe she was suffering from cancer.

Until the end of the Middle Ages, European Christians banned all surgery, as it was seen to be against their religion.

Some Stone Age jewellery was made from human teeth.

The few people who survived the ancient practice of *trepanation* (the removal of a piece of skull bone) would wear the bone as an amulet. Pretty!

When Alexander the Great was hit in the chest with an arrow, his general later wrote that 'his breath as well as his blood spouted from the wound'. He was describing a lung injury that is known today as a 'sucking chest wound'.

Gunpowder used to contain stale urine.

Scottish writer Sir Thomas Urquhart dropped dead during a fit of laughter. At least he died happy!

When he was a student, 16th-century Danish astronomer Tycho Brahe thought a swordfight in the dark would be a good idea. His nose was sliced off and he had to wear a false one for the rest of his life!

Early X-rays caused nasty side effects such as skin burns, swelling and hair loss.

The CIA devised hundreds of ways to kill Cuban leader Fidel Castro, including an exploding seashell, a cigar bomb and a contaminated wetsuit.

Head binding was practised in many ancient cultures to make the skull elongated, flat or conical shaped.

Robert Liston was the fastest surgeon in 19th-century Scotland – he could carry out an amputation in just 30 seconds.

Eighteenth-century British monarch Queen Anne had 18 children, but they all died before the age of 12.

During the Middle Ages, people thought that warts were the result of witches' spells.

Young British Prime Minister William Pitt the Younger was advised to drink a bottle of port a day to cure his gout…and instead died from liver damage at the age of 46.

The Bishop of Rochester's cook, disgruntled after an argument, got his revenge by poisoning the evening meal and giving two guests fatal diarrhoea. When Henry VIII found out, he was furious and ordered that the cook be boiled alive in his own pot!

King George II had a heart attack and died while he was on the toilet.

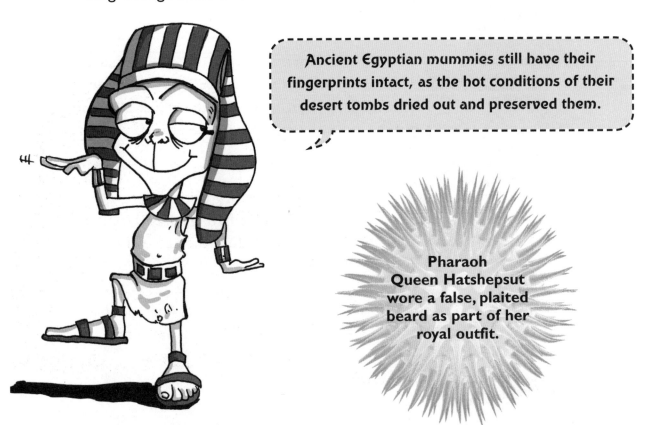

Ancient Egyptian mummies still have their fingerprints intact, as the hot conditions of their desert tombs dried out and preserved them.

Pharaoh Queen Hatshepsut wore a false, plaited beard as part of her royal outfit.

Many children who had to work in mines in the early 20th century lost their eyesight from being in darkness all day.

US President William Howard Taft was so overweight that he got stuck in the White House bath and it had to be replaced with a larger one.

Greek philosopher Socrates was condemned to execution by poisoning and had to swallow a drink made from the toxic plant *poison hemlock*, which causes death by paralysis.

Ancient Egyptians believed that bodily fluids such as tears and urine came from the heart.

Until the early 20th century, it was believed that life expectancy depended on heart rate; a slow heartbeat would give a longer life, so people thought that was why tortoises lived for so long.

In 1890, William Kemmler became the first criminal to be executed by the electric chair. Supposedly a quick new method, it took eight minutes and two attempts before he died.

Russian dictator Josef Stalin was twice run over by horse-drawn carriages as a boy, leaving him with a withered arm. He had bad smallpox scars, too.

Ancient Roman whips were especially vicious – they had pieces of bone or metal on the end.

One of the less pleasant jobs in the 18th century was a 'fart-catcher' – a footman who had to walk closely behind his master or mistress.

People have always had tooth decay – in ancient times, they believed that a 'tooth worm' ate the teeth and left holes behind.

Eighth-century Chinese poet Li Bai tried to touch the moon from a boat on the Yangtze River…but fell in and drowned.

Italian dictator Benito Mussolini's violent tendencies surfaced at an early age – he was expelled from school for stabbing a schoolmate's hand and poking a stick in another boy's eye.

Many ancient Greek Olympic events were carried out naked. Oo-er!

Rabies is an ancient disease that used to be so feared that people bitten by a rabid dog would kill themselves... before somebody else did!

Before embalming methods were developed, dead bodies that had to be transported over long distances would have the skin, muscles and organs cut away, leaving only the bones.

The cork false leg of 19th-century Mexican general Santa Anna was captured by US troops and is on display in a museum in Illinois.

The heart of English novelist Thomas Hardy is buried in Dorset, but his ashes are in Westminster Abbey.

During the 17th century, *tuberculosis* sufferers were suspected of being vampires! This was because they coughed-up blood and looked pale, with bloodshot eyes.

The *morning star* was a deadly medieval club-like weapon with big spikes on the end. Battling knights used it to whack and stab their enemies with one blow.

Ancient Egyptians used a special long-handled spoon to scoop out a corpse's brain – through the nose – before mummification.

An *oubliette* was a high-walled castle dungeon where prisoners were left to die of starvation. Workers who recently discovered the one in Leap Castle, Ireland, removed three cartloads of old human bones from it.

Ancient Indians inoculated themselves against *smallpox* by rubbing pus from an infected person into a scratch on their bodies.

Centuries ago, the way a guilty criminal was executed depended on his or her background – commoners were burned or hanged, while the more noble had the privilege of an 'honourable' death by decapitation with a sword!

English sporting hero C.B. Fry was said to be able to jump backwards from a stationary position and land on a mantelpiece.

Some ancient remedies did work. Wounds were often treated with honey and willow bark – honey is a natural antiseptic and willow contains the painkiller that is in aspirin.

A 16th-century treatment for baldness was to clean the head with a shampoo made from crushed beetles, then rub a nice bit of fox fat on it.

The fashionable tight corsets of the past were very bad for women's bodies, as they squished the liver, stomach and lungs so that they would not work properly.

Indian doctors used to stitch wounds with ants, by holding the skin closed and getting the ant to bite the join. The ant's head would then be snapped off, leaving its jaws as the stitch!

One symptom of *smallpox* was *black pox* – the skin took on a charred appearance, turning black and peeling off.

In the 19th century, London had a railway service for the dead! Mourners and coffin bearers would depart from Necropolis Station and get off at Cemetery Station, where the funerals were held in Brookwood Cemetery.

In a 1960s US army experiment to test the affects of panic on soldiers' behaviour, a planeload of men were told that they were about to crash. Surprisingly enough, the answers on their questionnaires didn't make a lot of sense…

Whenever stomach acid was needed for experiments, 18th-century Italian biologist Lazzaro Spallanzani would obligingly make himself sick to provide some.

The naked bodies in Michelangelo's paintings in the Sistine Chapel were considered too shocking, so another artist had to paint clothes over the offending parts.

More than 30 people have killed themselves by jumping from New York's Empire State Building.

Queen Elizabeth I had very bad teeth, but was so afraid of having one taken out that a loyal Archbishop had to have one of his teeth removed first to reassure her.

The Catherine wheel isn't just a pretty firework – it was a medieval execution device. Criminals would be tied to a wheel and bludgeoned until their bones broke. The really unlucky ones would be left out for the birds to feast on…

Ancient Greek prisoners condemned to death by the *brazen bull* were locked inside a brass sphere over a fire and roasted to death.

The dead bodies of poor people who couldn't afford funerals were often thrown in the nearest river. Dredger men didn't mind too much – they were paid for each corpse they collected.

Alexander the Great had clean-shaven soldiers so that their enemies couldn't grab hold of their beards during hand-to-hand combat.

Roman gladiators had to fight to the bitter end – any who stopped would be prodded with hot pokers to spur them on again.

French king Charles I was killed with a *halberd* – an axe on a pole that sliced through the helmet of his armour.

Maladies and Malfunctions

A *teratoma*, meaning 'monster tumour', is a rare growth inside the body, which can be a jumbled mass of hair, teeth, bone or even an eyeball!

The nail fungus *onychomycosis* can turn your nails green.

Australian footballer Daniel Chick got so fed up with the painful injury to his left ring finger that he asked to have it amputated.

Lungs are not able to get rid of coal dust. Miners may suffer from black lung disease, where a build-up of coal dust blackens and destroys the lungs, because the lungs cannot cough up the dust.

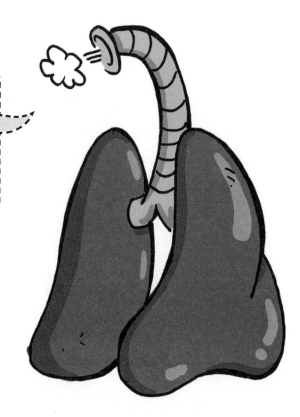

The painful eye infection *trachoma* is contagious and causes blindness, damaging the sight of around eight million people in the developing world.

When two-year-old Mackenzie Argaet had a liver transplant, there was one problem: the adult liver she received was too big. Her doctor used a novel idea to give it support and to stop it squashing vital blood vessels: he put in a ping pong ball!

Ever wondered why you salivate before throwing up? It's your body's way of protecting your teeth from the high acid levels in vomit.

Blackwater fever is so called because its sufferers pass black urine.

The rare phenomenon known as *Blaschko's lines* is characterized by pigmented stripes on a person's skin, particularly across the back.

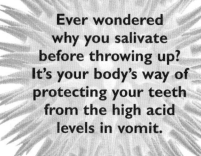

More people are allergic to cows' milk than to any other food or drink.

Babies born with the rare condition *craniofacial duplication* have one head but two faces.

Many World War I soldiers suffered from *trench mouth*, in which the gums became swollen and ulcerated. Left untreated, it spread to the cheeks, lips and jawbone.

A British man who was engulfed by clouds of mould when he opened compost in his garden suffered from acute *aspergillosis* – the spores invaded his lungs and damaged them so badly that he died.

A blockage in the bowel can lead to faecal vomiting, in which faeces are pushed back into the stomach from the colon and gush out of the mouth.

In some developing countries, there is a custom of dressing a newborn baby's umbilical cord stump with animal dung to stop it bleeding. This often leads to infection and the serious illness *tetanus*.

A bruise is a blood leak under your skin – a bigger leak makes a bigger bruise.

Women who wear very high heels too often, suffer from pain in the ball of the foot. There are now Botox 'foot filler' injections available that give sufferers built-in foot pads…or they could just stop wearing ridiculous shoes!

Ever heard of *monkeypox*? It's similar to chickenpox; the difference is that you catch monkeypox from monkeys, but you catch chickenpox from… humans!

The fungal infection *black hairy tongue* causes the taste buds to swell and discolour, giving the tongue a dark, furry appearance.

The tropical virus *dengue fever* causes such bad joint and muscle pains that it is also known as 'bonecrusher disease'.

People with the rare condition *Naegeli Syndrome* have no fingerprints.

Lung pinprick condition is a rare hereditary illness in which microscopic holes appear in the lungs, making people breathe louder than usual.

All the food debris, mucous and dead cells on your tongue are a playground for the bacteria that cause bad breath smells when they multiply.

Soldiers in tropical climates can suffer from *jungle rot*, a fungal infection that begins with sores on the feet and spreads to the rest of the body.

A head injury or earwax build-up can cause *tinnitus* – a ringing, whistling or hissing noise in one or both ears...all the time!

In a rare birth defect known as *congenital cystic* eye, a baby is born with a fluid-filled cyst in place of an eye.

The strange lumps on some rugby players' ears are known as *cauliflower ear*. They are caused by blood clots forming on the ear after being hit or by skin being torn from the ear's cartilage.

Conjunctivitis is a fairly common infection that makes the eyes red, itchy and gunky. It's highly contagious, too…

If a person's liver isn't working properly, their hands can swell up so that the fingers look like fat sausages. The condition is known as *clubbing*.

There is no cure for the common cold, as there are hundreds of viruses that cause it.

American banjo player Eddie Adcock developed a hand tremor that affected his playing. To stop it, surgeons operated on his brain…while he was still awake and strumming on his banjo!

The middle ear is filled with air so that the ear bones can move freely to process sounds. *Glue ear* is when the ear fills with goo instead, which dulls the hearing but is surprisingly painless!

Singer Christopher Sands had a bout of hiccups that lasted for 15 months! He was finally cured by an operation to replace a faulty valve in his stomach.

People with the enzyme deficiency *methemoglobinemia* have blue skin, as their blood carries much less oxygen than it should. Oxygenated blood is bright red and gives white skin its pink colour.

If the delicate blood vessels in the eye membrane are ruptured, a bright red haemorrhage will spread across the white of the eye.

During a severe ear infection, the eardrum may burst to allow all the built-up pus to seep out.

Damage to the lower part of the brain can result in *locked-in syndrome*: the sufferer is paralysed, but is fully aware of what is going on around them and can communicate only through eye movements and blinking.

Bad breath doesn't just come from the mouth – a sinus infection can make whiffy air come out of the nose!

A severe case of the vitamin deficiency disease *pellagra* is characterized by 'the four d's': diarrhoea, dermatitis, dementia and death.

Rat-bite fever is caught from rodent bites or rodent urine and causes a high temperature, headache, vomiting and agonizing joint pains.

One form of tinnitus isn't just in the head! Ear muscle spasms can make clicking or crackling sounds that can be heard by anyone else listening nearby.

Swollen hands are an occupational hazard for boxers, but Ukrainian boxer Vitali Klitschko has his own remedy – baby pee! He reckons that his son's wet nappies reduce the swelling when he wraps them around his fists after a match.

Smallpox is the only human infectious disease to have been eradicated through vaccination.

During a really bad nosebleed, blood can rush through the sinuses and squirt out of the eyes.

Someone with *hypertrichosis*, or Werewolf Syndrome, has extra long hair all over their body, including their face.

Many sailors of the past died from vitamin C deficiency, known as *scurvy* – they would first suffer from spongy gums, loose teeth, weakness and purple blotches on the skin.

Scientific tests showed that a protein secreted by bullfrogs could wipe out **MRSA**, one of the nasty 'superbugs' that lurk in some hospitals.

According to the World Health Organization, 75 per cent of the world's blindness could be prevented or treated.

People with *microcephaly* have heads that are much smaller than average.

Deadly anthrax spores can lay dormant in soil for centuries.

According to the charity Cancer Research UK, one in three people will get cancer at some time in their life.

The *mumps* virus causes painful swelling of the salivary glands and gives sufferers puffed-out 'hamster cheeks'.

Chinese man Huang Chungcai suffers from severe *neurofibromatosis*, a genetic disorder that leads to the growth of nerve tissue tumours. He has had two operations to remove tumours from his face, which weighed a total of 20 kilograms/44 pounds – the same weight as 20 bags of sugar.

Tinea cruris is a fungal infection around the groin. It often affects sportspeople, so its other name is 'jock itch'!

Smoking is bad for your teeth! Smokers are at a higher risk of getting *periodontitis,* which makes the bone around the teeth wear away until they loosen and fall out.

A US study showed that there is an 18 per cent increase in fatal road accidents on presidential election days.

Pus is a gooey yellow cocktail of dead cells, bacteria, proteins and white blood cells.

Brain diseases known as *spongiform encephalopathies* cause the brain to become riddled with holes, so it looks like a sponge.

Sonic booms are produced when military jets break the sound barrier whilst flying at low altitude. They are painful to the ears and can even cause nosebleeds, so have been used as weapons in warfare.

The swollen 'glands' that you get when you're ill are actually your lymph nodes – they can swell to the size of an orange when they're fighting an infection.

A person suffering from *tonsillitis* can get *quinsy* – a painful abscess in the throat that makes swallowing impossible.

There are more than 200 types of cancer.

The deadly Ebola virus makes sufferers throw-up thick, black vomit.

Fatal insomnia **is a rare inherited illness that is incurable – sufferers get so little sleep that their bodies begin to shut down and they eventually die of exhaustion.**

Pet reptiles may seem like fun, but they can be hazardous – nine out of ten reptiles have the salmonella bacteria in their faeces, which can be passed on to owners and cause serious illness.

Being struck by lightning is a huge body shock – it can leave a person with perforated eardrums, burns, cataracts and paralysis. So if there's an electrical storm, stay inside!

Around 40 per cent of brain tumours are benign (non-cancerous).

The cancerous bladder that killed Italian biologist Lazzaro Spallanzani is on display in a museum in Pavia.

Zygomycosis is a nasty fungal infection that spreads through the body super-fast and leads to headaches, black nose discharge, swollen eyes and rotting of the flesh.

During laser eye surgery, a cut is made in the eye and a laser is used to change the shape of the cornea...while the patient is awake!

Vibration white finger is a painful condition that affects people working with vibrating machinery, such as drills or chainsaws. The blood supply to the fingers and toes becomes restricted, in extreme cases leading to ulcers and gangrene.

Penny-pinching US multi-millionairess Hetty Green would not pay for her son to have his broken leg treated. He then got gangrene and had to have the limb amputated.

Acne is not contagious and is not affected by whether the skin is clean or not – in fact, too much washing can make it worse.

Many more men than women are colour-blind – around one in 12.

The infection *thrush* causes a white fungus to sprout all over the tongue.

Cradle cap is the crusty, yellow, scaly stuff on a young baby's scalp. You might think it looks yucky, but it doesn't bother the baby!

The lung disease *tuberculosis* kills around three million people worldwide every year – more than any other infectious illness.

Most bacteria and viruses that invade your body have evolved to be most effective at 37 degrees Celsius/98.6 degrees Fahrenheit. A fever is your body's way of killing them off!

The deadly poison *strychnine* causes dramatic muscle spasms throughout the body until the back arches and breathing stops.

A car accident victim from Nottinghamshire, England, was impaled by a snooker cue that had been in the car's boot. It missed her vital organs and she was released from hospital just three days later.

The rare skin infection *necrotising fasciitis* produces toxins that destroy skin and muscle. Large open wounds form and sometimes amputation of the affected part is necessary.

Someone with the rare condition *aniridia* has no *irises* (the coloured part of the eye), so their eyes look completely black, like big pupils.

A stroke is caused by blocked or burst blood vessels in the brain.

Indian girl Lakshmi Tatma was born attached to a headless parasitic twin so that she had an extra pair of arms and legs. Thirty doctors worked for 24 hours to perform the successful operation to remove her spare limbs.

A high fever can cause an unpleasant sensation called *formication* – it feels as if ants are crawling all over your skin!

Tetanus causes facial spasms and stops the mouth opening, which is why the disease is also known as 'lockjaw'.

Mouth ulcers that are more than 1 centimetre/half an inch wide are known as *major aphthous ulcerations*. The minor ones are bad enough!

Some people are allergic to mobile phones! A person with a nickel allergy will develop a rash when their skin comes into contact with any buttons or handsets that are made from the metal.

Surfing the internet boosts brainpower! A University of California study showed that using the web stimulates the decision-making and reasoning parts of the brain.

New Zealand celebrity Lana Coc-Kroft went into a coma for two weeks after injuring her foot on some coral and contracting *toxic shock syndrome*, a rare disease caused by toxic bacteria.

A lightning strike can rupture blood capillaries on the skin and create red, snaky patterns, known as *lightning flowers*.

Ankylosing spondylitis is a painful spine condition that can lead to a permanent stooping posture.

The skin infection *ringworm* has no worms in it – just fungus!

Sufferers of *stiff person syndrome* experience sudden muscle spasms that can be triggered by noise or stress.

People with *anosmia* have no sense of smell and very little sense of taste. This not only makes life a little dull, it can be dangerous – they can't smell signs of danger, such as smoke or gas.

Verrucas that grow in clusters are known as *mosaic warts*.

An Iranian woman's grounds for divorce were that her husband was just disgusting – he hadn't washed for over a year!

Some plants, such as poison ivy, contain a skin-irritating resin – just brushing against them will give you a stinging, blistery rash.

More obese people in the world means bigger coffins – one British council had to install extra large furnaces in its crematoriums to accommodate 1-metre/3-feet wide coffins.

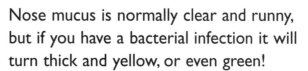

Space sickness is the mother of all motion sickness – the lack of gravity confuses the brain, causing headaches, nausea, loss of balance and feelings of confusion.

Someone with *cutaneous anthrax* will have large, black ulcers on their skin.

Nose mucus is normally clear and runny, but if you have a bacterial infection it will turn thick and yellow, or even green!

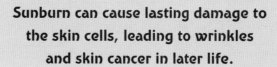

Sunburn can cause lasting damage to the skin cells, leading to wrinkles and skin cancer in later life.

Some infections can produce blue pus! The freaky colour comes from *pseudomonas* bacteria.

Severe vomiting can burst the blood vessels around the eyes and cause a black eye.

So little blood reaches the extremities in subzero temperatures that frostbite is a hazard for mountaineers – fingers or toes that rot and go black must be amputated.

A study of British people travelling to work on public transport showed that one in four of them had faecal bacteria on their hands. That's poop germs to the rest of us. Ewww!

Indonesian fisherman Dede Koswara suffers from a rare genetic disorder – his body reacted to a wart virus by covering his skin with huge growths that look like tree bark.

Tinea barbae, also known as 'barber's itch', is a fungal infection that affects a man's beard area, producing painful swellings around the hair roots on the cheeks and chin.

You were probably inoculated against *polio* when you were younger, but the paralysing disease still exists in four countries in the world: India, Nigeria, Pakistan and Afghanistan.

Cash-strapped health authorities in Germany couldn't afford the specially adapted ambulances needed to transport obese patients, so they used cattle trucks instead!

The body of a Canadian man became mummified in the hot, dry conditions at the time of his death – there was no smell to alert neighbours, so it was two years before he was found.

Someone with *Cushing's syndrome* will become obese, whatever they eat.

A lack of the mineral *iodine* in the diet makes the thyroid gland swell up, creating a large lump in the neck known as a *goitre*.

A liver damaged by the disease *cirrhosis* is orangey-yellow and knobbly.

Blisters are squidgy because they're full of lymph and other body fluids.

More than 40,000 droplets are sprayed into the air when you sneeze. If you have any infectious germs, it's a very effective way of spreading them…

Exploding head syndrome isn't quite as gruesome as it sounds – it's a severe form of tinnitus, making sufferers hear a terrifyingly loud explosion or gunshot whilst falling asleep.

US man Kenneth Bromley became so obese that doctors had to remove 95 kilograms/210 pounds of fat from his legs and abdomen.

When medics were called to take Florida woman Gayle Grinds to hospital, they found that she was stuck to her couch – after spending six years on it, the obese woman's skin had fused with the fabric.

Once you've had a cold sore, the virus that causes it lurks in your body for life and can pop back up at any time.

One symptom of *scarlet fever* is *strawberry tongue* – the tongue swells up and turns bright red, making it look like a strawberry.

A damaged cornea can be replaced in a straightforward cornea transplant operation, but the new cornea has to come from a fresh corpse.

Russian Alexander Sizonenko can't stop growing! The former basketball player suffers from *gigantism* and was 8 feet/2.44 metres tall when last measured.

The toxic chemicals in 10 kilograms/22 pounds of chocolate would kill you...but you couldn't eat all that without vomiting anyway!

British man William McIloy had 400 operations...that he didn't need! He had the mental disorder *Munchausen syndrome*, which makes people fake severe illness to get medical attention.

A bad gum infection called *gingivitis* can lead to pus-filled mouth sores, purple gums and the stinkiest of stinky breath.

One in 100,000 babies is born with *sirenomelia*, or 'mermaid syndrome', in which the legs are fused together and look like a mermaid's tail.

The black dot in the middle of a verruca is its blood supply.

Cataracts are the most common cause of blindness in the world.

When footballer Paulo Diogo tried to jump over a barrier during a goal celebration, his wedding ring got caught and he lost the top half of his finger. The referee even gave him a yellow card for wasting time!

Snow blindness occurs when the eyes are sunburnt from the strong sunlight reflected off snow or ice. The eyes become swollen and painful, and in extreme cases people can go blind.

Liquid nitrogen causes instant frostbite on healthy skin, but is often used to destroy the abnormal skin cells that make up warts and moles.

Obstipation is severe, agonising constipation.

A person with *Hurler syndrome* has a face like a gargoyle's.

The hereditary disorder *haemochromatosis* makes the body absorb too much iron, seriously damaging the organs and turning the skin a bronze colour.

Deafness in old age could be down to a lifetime of noise. A study of African tribesmen who had never been exposed to transport noise showed that they all had good hearing, regardless of age.

Nasal polyps are fleshy growths in the nostril that can affect the sense of smell – a big one can be the size of a grape!

Entropion is a condition in which the eyelid turns inwards and rubs against the eyeball. If left untreated, it causes an ulcer and can lead to blindness.

Carbuncles are skin abscesses that can be as big as golf balls and ooze pus from one or two openings – and they're contagious!

A major zit invasion can turn into _cystic acne_, where the spots grow larger and become swollen, painful and pus-filled.

Syndactyly is the term used for webbed hands or feet.

In 2008, Chinese milk products contaminated with the industrial chemical melamine caused kidney problems that were sometimes fatal – more than 90,000 people became ill and four babies died.

Some ear infections make you throw up! Viruses that affect the inner ear can alter your sense of balance and make you feel seasick.

At the age of four, Australian Sam Carpenter caught his hand in a meat mincer at his father's butcher's shop. Half of his arm had to be amputated, but he went on to become a professional footballer.

After 30 years of smelling like stale fish, a 41 year-old Australian woman finally had her rare disorder diagnosed – *trimethylaminuria* is also known as 'fish malodour syndrome' and affects the smell of sweat, breath and urine.

Plugged-up sweat glands cause prickly heat rash in hot weather – fresh sweat gets trapped and forms a prickling, itchy rash of tiny blisters.

Some people react to bright sunlight by sneezing. This is called *photic sneezing* and is inherited, so you can blame your parents if it happens to you!

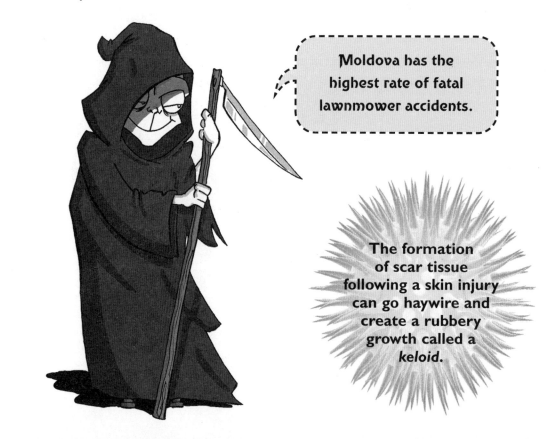

Moldova has the highest rate of fatal lawnmower accidents.

The formation of scar tissue following a skin injury can go haywire and create a rubbery growth called a *keloid*.

Record-breaking Bodies

Japanese super-skipper Megumi Suzuki can skip rope 152 times in 30 seconds.

US man Doug Williams had a freaky nipple hair that was 12.7 centimetres/5 inches long. He reckons a cheeseburger a day is what made that hair grow so well!

One of Napoleon Bonaparte's teeth became the most valuable ever when it was sold at auction in Wiltshire, England, for £11,000/US$15,500. The French General's upper right canine tooth was taken out when he had scurvy and his mouth became infected.

Top sniffer Madeline Albrecht smelled at least 5,600 feet during her 15 years as a hygiene product tester, more than anyone else on the planet. She had to stick her nose in thousands of armpits, too!

In 2008, Ethiopian athlete Haile Gebrselassie broke all previous marathon records when he ran the 42-kilometre/26-mile Berlin marathon in 2 hours 3 minutes 59 seconds.

Chinese doctor Wei Shengchu set a record in 2004 when he had 1,790 acupuncture needles stuck into his head and face.

One of the world's tallest men is Mongolian herdsman Bao Xishun, who is 2.4 metres/7 feet 9 inches tall. He became the world's tallest father in October 2008 with the arrival of his son.

Your shoulder joint is the most mobile joint in your body. The bad news is that it's also the easiest joint to dislocate!

Brazilian star striker Ronaldo has scored more World Cup Final goals than any other footballer – 15 in total.

Eighteenth-century circus attraction Thomas Wedders had the biggest nose ever: it was 19 centimetres/7.5 inches long!

US man W.R. 'Rusty' Haight crashes cars for a living! He has been a 'human crash-test dummy' in a record 846 collisions.

To stop small boys being used as jockeys in camel racing, the Qatar government asked a Swiss company to invent robot jockeys that look – and even smell – like children!

By the time she retired, twinkle-toed US soccer player Mia Hamm had scored 158 international goals – more than any other player in the sport's history.

Darren Taylor is a master of the belly flop: he is able to keep his body horizontal to land safely in just 30 centimetres/12 inches of water from a height of over 10 metres/30 feet. Don't try it yourself!

The name of the lung disease *pneumonoultramicroscopicsilicovolcanoconiosis* is the longest word in the English language.

African Johannes Relleke was attacked by bees in 1962 and had 2,443 stings removed.

Motorcycle daredevil Evel Knievel broke a record 433 bones during his many stunts.

Around 80 per cent of adults who live in the South Pacific island nation of Nauru are obese, giving it the highest obesity rate in the world.

The odds of being struck once by lightning are 3,000 to 1, but US park ranger Roy C Sullivan survived being struck seven times!

As of 2009, US swimmer Michael Phelps has won 14 Olympic gold medals – more than any other Olympic athlete.

The largest object ever removed from a skull was a 46-centimetre/18-inch long drill bit, after US construction worker Ron Hunt fell off a ladder and landed face first on to it. He lost an eye but escaped brain damage and made a full recovery.

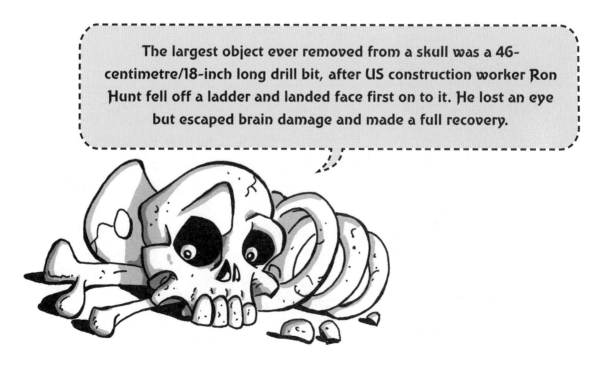

British hula-hooper Leah Black managed 162 hula revolutions in one minute. Grab your own hoop and see how many you can do!

British man Dave Cornthwaite travelled across Australia, from Perth to Brisbane…on a skateboard! His 5,823-kilometre/3,618-mile trip was the longest skateboard journey ever.

US man Milburn Hart did a parachute jump at the age of 96 years 63 days. Go, Grandad, go!

US sisters Anne and Claire Recht are the world's tallest female twins – both are more than 2.01 metres/6 feet 7 inches tall.

The Gomez family from Mexico is the world's hairiest family – the men have 98 per cent of their bodies covered in long hair.

Chinese badminton player Fu Haifeng has a powerful serving arm – he can send a shuttlecock whizzing through the air at 332 kilometres/206 miles an hour.

How many tennis balls can you hold in one hand? Frenchman Arnaud Deschamps held 19 – for 10 whole seconds!

After losing her arm in a motorcycle accident, US woman Claudia Mitchell became the first woman to receive a bionic arm, which she can control by thought alone.

The longest coma lasted for 37 years – Elaine Esposito died at the age of 43 after sinking into unconsciousness following an operation as a child.

Corset queen Cathie Jung has deformed her body in the way Victorians used to, so that she has a corseted waist measurement of just 38.1 centimetres/15 inches.

Jamaican athlete Usain 'Lightning' Bolt ran the 100 metres in a record-breaking 9.69 seconds at the Beijing Olympics. Physicists reckon he could have been even quicker if he hadn't started his celebration before he reached the finish line!

New Zealander Lucky Diamond Rich is tattooed on every inch of his body, including his gums and inside his ears. He even has tattoos on his tattoos!

American woman Carol McFadden has been collecting earrings since 1952 and now has more than 37,700 pairs. Even if she wore two pairs each day, it would take more than 50 years to wear them all just once!

At the age of 26 years and 244 days, Karen Zacharias from the US became the youngest person ever to complete a marathon on all seven continents.

Finger-wrestling contests have been held in Bavaria since the 14th century, longer than anywhere else in the world.

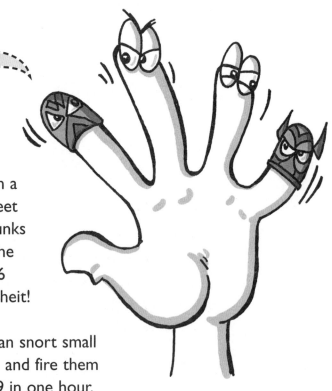

'Iceman' Wim Hof spent more than a minute swimming 57 metres/188 feet under ice in nothing more than trunks and goggles. The temperature of the water was a body-numbing minus 6 degrees Celsius/21 degrees Fahrenheit!

Indian yoga guru GP Vijayakumar can snort small fish through the back of his mouth and fire them out of his nostril. His record is 509 in one hour.

Lake Nyos in Cameroon, West Africa, is the world's deadliest lake. Occasional releases of naturally produced carbon dioxide suffocate people and animals nearby – more than 1,600 people were killed in one night in 1986.

See how long you can make a basketball spin on your finger and try beating Joseph Odjiambo's record of 4 hours and 15 minutes!

Zookeeping graduate 'Jungle' John LaMedica holds the record for sharing a coffin with the most cockroaches – he had 20,050 giant Madagascan hissing cockroaches crawling all over his body in 1999. Still no challengers, then?

The oldest person on record was Frenchwoman Jeanne Calment, who was 122 years and 164 days old when she died.

US woman Lee Redmond has not cut her nails since 1979, so they now have a total length of 7.51 metres/24 feet 7 inches.

Nine-year-old Sandeep Kaur had the first ever full-face replant operation in 1994, after her face and scalp were ripped off when her pigtails got caught in a threshing machine. The operation was successful and she grew up to become a nurse.

American Cecil Walker gulped down eight sausages in one minute by swallowing them whole! No doubt he then had to do the same with indigestion tablets...

French entertainer Monsieur Mangetout had the world's strangest diet – he spent a lifetime eating weird stuff, including bicycles, shopping trolleys and televisions. Bananas made him sick, though!

'Texas Snake Man' Jackie Bibby sat in a bathtub with 87 venomous rattlesnakes for 45 minutes. His trick was to keep very still!

Human extinguisher Antti Karvinen put out 36 flaming torches with his mouth in one minute in 2000.

German entertainer Patrick Brumbach threw a record 96 knives around a human target in one minute.

Kung Fu expert Dong Changsheng pulled a car along using ropes attached to…his lower eyelids!

Ben Cook from the US has the fastest thumbs in the west – he texted 160 characters in 42.2 seconds.

British schoolgirl Tiana Walton had 25 snails stuck on her face at once, breaking the previous record of 15. She said the slimy creatures were 'a bit cold' and 'quite smelly'.

British man Gordon Mattinson can contort his face so alarmingly that he has won the World Gurning Championships ten times!

In 24 hours, New Zealand cyclist Ken Looi rode 378.7 kilometres/235.3 miles…on a unicycle!

Strongman Muhamed Kahrimanovic, from Bosnia-Herzegovina, smashed 65 coconuts in one minute…using just his hands!

The oldest person to grow a new tooth was 61!

New Zealand's Ongaonga tree nettle is the most dangerous stinging plant in the world – even touching it lightly causes a painful sting that lasts for days, and falling into its toxic needle-like hairs can be fatal.

Monster saltwater crocodiles killed 9,980 Japanese soldiers who tried to cross Burmese mangrove swamps in 1945, making it the worst crocodile attack ever.

The length of an average appendix is around 10 centimetres/4 inches, but the largest ever was removed from a Croatian man and measured 26 centimetres/10.2 inches long!

Lithuanian beardy man Antanas Kontrimas holds the record for the heaviest weight lifted by a beard – he used his face fuzz to lift a girl weighing 63 kilograms/138 pounds.

In 2006, 594 couples gathered in Paris to kiss at the same time. Ooh, la la!

The oldest bride ever was Australian Minnie Munro, who was 102 when she tied the knot. Her groom was a nice young man of 82!

Australian Andrew Hajinikitas drank a record 120 millilitres/4.2 fluid ounces of tongue-obliterating Tabasco Sauce in 30 seconds.

If you fancy doing your own rocket jaunt, you could follow in the vapour trail of Iranian businesswoman Anousheh Ansari, the first female space tourist. She paid US$20 million/£14 million for the privilege!

Here's one you can try at home – test your lungs and see how far you can blow a malteser along with one breath through a straw! Wayne Iles managed 3.36 metres/11 feet.

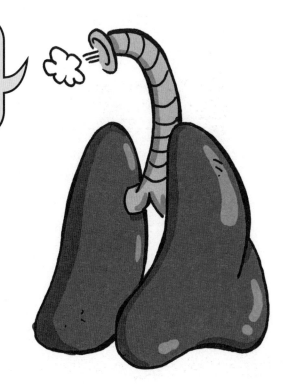

In 1972, US astronauts Eugene Cernan and Harrison Schmitt went on the longest moonwalk, taking more than seven hours to explore 20.4 kilometres/12.6 miles of the moon's surface.

Aerial stuntman Mike Howard walked on a beam between two hot air balloons 6,522 metres/21,400 feet above the ground – and he wasn't even wearing a parachute!

When Indian farmer Sanju Bhagat complained of stomach pains, the doctors who operated found his underdeveloped twin lodged in his abdomen! The half-formed twin, who had feet and hands, had been inside him for a record 36 years.

South African Lionel Lewis has donated a record 177 litres/376 pints of blood.

The loudest snore ever recorded was 93 decibels – that's louder than a car engine!

Nineteen scuba divers took part in the largest underwater cycle race, in Guernsey in 2005.

US man Dean Sheldon held an 18-centimetre/7-inch-long emperor scorpion in his mouth for 18 seconds.

French daredevil Alain Robert has climbed more than 85 towers, monuments and skyscrapers... without any equipment! No wonder his nickname is Spider-Man...

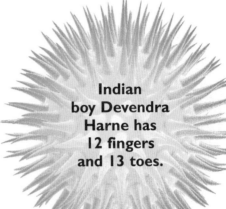

Indian boy Devendra Harne has 12 fingers and 13 toes.

The most expensive bar of soap was made using fat from Italian Prime Minister Silvio Berlusconi, and sold for US$18,000/£12,800.

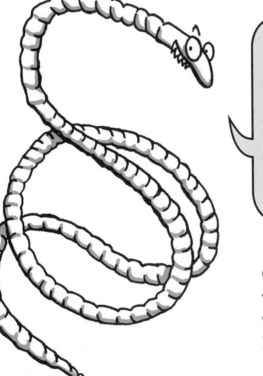

The largest parasite that infects humans is the fish tapeworm. It can live for up to 20 years and one adult worm sheds up to a million eggs a day – the biggest one ever recorded was 18 metres/60 feet long!

Canadian Ana Yang made the world's largest soap bubble, which was big enough to fit 26 people inside!

A crowd of 18,788 Portuguese women formed the largest ever human flag to show support for their national football team in 2006.

American bearded lady Vivian Wheeler gave up shaving in 1993 – seven years later, her facial hair had reached a record 27.9 centimetres/11 inches.

The deadliest natural toxin comes from bad food: *clostridium botulinum* is more poisonous than arsenic or snake venom and causes the deadly paralysing illness *botulism*.

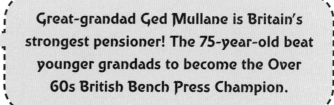

Great-grandad Ged Mullane is Britain's strongest pensioner! The 75-year-old beat younger grandads to become the Over 60s British Bench Press Champion.

Indian man Anthony Victor has the longest ear hair in the world, measuring 18.1 centimetres/7.12 inches.

'Rubber Boy' Daniel Browning Smith is known to be the most flexible man alive – he can dislocate his arms and legs to squeeze through a tennis racket in just 15 seconds!

Austrian Christian Rijavec somersaulted 29 times in 10 minutes...whilst skiing!

How many pairs of shoelaces can you tie in one minute? British man Andy Akinwolere managed 14, without getting his fingers in a twist!

If you can't be bothered to carve your own pumpkin next Hallowe'en, try asking Stephen Clarke for a helping hand – he's so fast with a knife that he can carve 42 pumpkins in an hour.

US woman Cindy Jackson has had more cosmetic surgery than anyone else in the world – 12 full-scale beauty operations and hundreds of minor procedures.

The brain removed from an US man in 1992 weighed 2.3 kilograms/5 pounds 1 ounce – almost twice as much as an average brain.

A record 13,380 people gathered at the Cuscatlán Stadium in El Salvador, South America, so that they could all brush their teeth at the same time!

The most powerful muscle in your body is the *masseter*, one of your chewing muscles. You have one on each side of the mouth and they're so strong that you could bite through a metal chain; unfortunately, your teeth would break before you managed it!

Canadian Aaron Gregg made 86 catches when he juggled with three running chainsaws...and he still had all his limbs intact!

Adventurous British teenager Jordan Maguire was just 14 when he walked to the North Pole from an air base in Russia, covering 178 kilometres/111 miles in ten days.

How many people can you fit into a Mini? Twenty-two is the record – but they didn't look too comfortable.

US man Frank Salvatore can balance a tower of 18 milk crates on his chin!

Before sensible boxing rules were introduced, Jack Jones and Patsy Tunney beat each other to a pulp in a fight that had 276 rounds and lasted a record 4 hours 30 minutes!

Kidney stones can form in the kidney and make a person ill. The most ever removed from one kidney was 728, which took three hours to remove!

The world's most premature surviving baby, Amillia Taylor, weighed 280 grams/10 ounces and was just the length of a ballpoint pen when she was born at less than 22 weeks.

Nepalese mountaineering guide Appa Sherpa has climbed to the top of Mount Everest a record 18 times.

British performer Scott Bell has super tough soles – he has walked 100 metres/ 328 feet over burning hot embers.

American Zach Warren completed the Philadelphia marathon in three hours, seven minutes, five seconds… and juggled all the way. The fastest juggling marathon ever!